Praise for *The Undercover Edge*

"Derrick channels years on the street in law enforcement into his new how-to book on communicating more effectively, leading with confidence, and battling life's obstacles head-on! Incredible!"

—Nancy Grace, TV personality and founder of CrimeOnLine.com

"Levasseur gives readers an incredibly insightful way to identify and achieve their goals in *The Undercover Edge*. Not only is his writing style engaging and illuminating, it is fundamentally practical and easy to understand. So easy, everyone can apply his ideas in their everyday lives or business ventures. When I read it, I was amazed at how Levasseur instinctively developed skills it took me decades to learn and hone as an FBI profiler. *The Undercover Edge* is pure genius!"

—Jim Clemente, FBI supervisory special agent and profiler

"Derrick Levasseur walks the reader through his law enforcement career and highlights tips and techniques that can be used by everyday people to gain new insights into social and business encounters. His conversational writing style makes the book easy to read and understand."

—Jack Schafer, PhD, author of *The Like Switch*

"For anyone who, like me, watched Derrick deftly maneuver his way to the grand prize on Big Brother and asked in amazement, 'How did he do that?' this book is the answer. From visualization to knowing your target to developing your intuition, Derrick breaks down a clear, practical, effective strategy for achieving your own goals in life. As entertaining and clever as his *Big Brother* run, *The Undercover Edge* will inspire you, motivate you, and put you directly on the path to becoming the person you want to be."

—Mandy Hale, *New York Times* bestselling author
of *The Single Woman* and *Beautiful Uncertainty*

"Levasseur's fresh and candid perspective makes for an empowering self-help guide."

—*Publishers Weekly*

THE
UNDERCOVER
EDGE

THE
UNDERCOVER
EDGE

FIND YOUR HIDDEN STRENGTHS, *LEARN* TO ADAPT, AND *BUILD* THE CONFIDENCE TO *WIN* LIFE'S GAME

DERRICK LEVASSEUR

sourcebooks

Published by Sourcebooks, Inc.
P.O. Box 4410, Naperville, Illinois 60567-4410
(630) 961-3900
Fax: (630) 961-2168
sourcebooks.com

The Library of Congress has cataloged the hardcover edition as follows:

Names: Levasseur, Derrick, author.
Title: The undercover edge : redefine the rules to win life's game / Derrick
  Levasseur.
Description: Naperville, Illinois : Sourcebooks, Inc., [2018] | Includes
  bibliographical references.
Identifiers: LCCN 2017023607 | (alk. paper)
Subjects: LCSH: Success. | Undercover operations.
Classification: LCC BF637.S8 L4465 2018 | DDC 650.1--dc23 LC record avail-
able at https://lccn.loc.gov/2017023607

Printed and bound in Canada.
MBP 10 9 8 7 6 5 4 3 2 1

To the three most important people in
my life: Jana, Tenley, and Peyton.

Thank you for your love and support. You are
the driving force behind everything I do.

CONTENTS

||||||||||||||||||||||||||||||||||||||||||||||||||||||||||||||

THE TRUTH

I have to admit, this is a surreal moment for me. Full disclosure: I never envisioned myself as an author. In my mind, I'm just a normal guy who had the opportunity to work as an undercover detective at a very young age. Sure, I've had friends and acquaintances tell me I should write about my career, my personal life, and my stint on reality television. But I wouldn't write a book just to talk about what I've accomplished. The only reason I would take the time to put my thoughts on paper was if I felt I had something important to contribute, something that could benefit other people. After all, that's why I originally got into law enforcement—to help others.

I can assure you that I don't do anything half-heartedly, so the fact that you're seeing my words on this page means that I *do* feel I have information that could be beneficial to you. About three years ago, I realized that my approach to interacting with people wasn't just who I was or "Derrick being Derrick." The totality of circumstances throughout my life has led me to become the person I am today. It's also the reason I evaluate and communicate with others in the way that I do. My specialized law-enforcement training and on-the-job experiences, coupled with social encounters outside of work, have created an effective approach to dealing with people that I use every day. Going undercover taught me how to define my goals, lead my team more effectively, and build confidence in my actions both in the rarest and in the more common everyday challenges. This isn't a single tactic or technique I employ. For me, it's a way of life.

So the question is, how do I teach *you* the same approach? Should I have you apply to the police academy? Become an undercover detective? Put you in life-threatening situations where the wrong choice of words could get you killed? No, I think I have a better idea, and it's a whole lot safer. In this book, I have taken my thirteen years of training and experience and condensed it into a series of lessons that will show you how I applied this knowledge to all aspects of my life.

I should probably explain who I am and what I bring to the table before we get down to business. When I was officially sworn in as a police officer, I was only twenty years old, making me one of the youngest in my department's history. As soon as I graduated from the police academy and started my career as a patrolman, my supervisors noticed that in addition to being young, I had a way with words, so I was recruited to work undercover.

I remember getting the call from the chief of police for my first operation. This is the top guy in any department and not someone a patrolman like myself usually hears from personally. It was the morning after my twenty-first birthday. Now, I'm not going to lie: I had a few celebratory drinks the night before, and I was a little under the weather. But as soon as I realized what he was asking me to do, I woke right up. Later that very day, I posed as a college student at a major university, and when it was all said and done, we made multiple arrests and seized a large amount of drugs.

After that experience, I was hooked. I knew I had found my calling. Undercover work came naturally to me, and I was able to adapt to most environments fairly easily. Over the years, I worked for multiple agencies, posing as a student, a drug dealer, a drug user, and several other characters.

You might be thinking, "Wow, that must have been a lot of fun." Well, in many ways it was, but when you get right down to what the job actually entailed—like finding yourself alone in a room with a bunch of criminals—it was also very dangerous. I risked being discovered by the people I was trying to build a case against, and in many instances, these were bad people with a lot to lose. So it goes without saying that I've been in some scary situations.

I'm excited for the opportunity to explain what I've learned during my time as a street cop, an undercover detective, and a sergeant. Very few people are aware of the information that investigators learn during the various schools we attend throughout our career. The purpose of this training is to keep us updated on the latest trends and techniques and how we can use them to our advantage. I'm convinced that once you obtain the knowledge I have gained during my training, you'll also enjoy many of the advantages it gave me both personally and professionally. The good news is that you're going to learn the same approach that I learned without exposing yourself to any of the life-threatening dangers that I faced—allowing you to reap the rewards without the risk.

Police work is a lot like human chess. Of course, it's not an actual game; it's serious stuff and can have some real consequences. But still, the analogy holds true. In *The Undercover Edge*, we're going to go over a lot of information that will help you understand where people are coming from and why they do the things they do. Some of this may also help you better understand yourself, and why you do some of the things *you* do, which can assist in planning your next move.

I know there's one question that a perceptive reader will have at this point, and that is, "Why should I care about what you've learned as a detective or supervisor? What relevance could that kind of training have for me in the non-law-enforcement world?"

First off, I cannot stress this point enough: this is not a book for someone who wants to become a detective. Yes, if you have aspirations to be in law enforcement, there's a lot of information in this book that will help you improve your skills. However, I have adapted this approach to work for whatever profession you're in. And a lot of the experiences I had while working as cop are in this book because the insight I gained during those interactions is just as effective in normal, everyday social encounters. Actually, some of the techniques I implemented at work, like visualizing my actions before carrying them out, were derived from my childhood, making them applicable in almost any situation. Without holding anything back, I'm going to share all the details associated with these practices so that you can incorporate them into *your* life.

It's also worth noting that while working as a detective, I didn't want to be perceived as one-dimensional. I had aspirations to work for the FBI, so I went back to school and completed my master's degree in business management. Although my intent was to diversify my abilities, grad school also changed my perspective on leadership. If there's one thing I've learned about a police department in comparison to a private business, it's that the objectives may be different but the core principals, such as infrastructure and the operations of the administration, are the same.

Although I gained some insight while attending school, certain things can't be taught; they have to be experienced. I've had a lot of success throughout my career, but I've also seen a lot of tragedy, none of which I would wish upon anyone. I was only twenty-three years old when I was involved in a shooting with a man who tried to kill me. I was left with no other choice but to shoot him, and unfortunately, he did not survive his injuries. It was definitely traumatic, and I did a lot of soul-searching over the next eight months. I still reflect back on it to this day. Do you think I learned anything about myself from that experience? Absolutely. Was what I learned more about "Derrick the person" and less about "Derrick the cop"? Of course it was, and what I took away from that incident is beneficial to everyone, not just a police officer.

I will say this: I'm not a millionaire or a famous entrepreneur. If that's what you're looking for, I'm not your guy. But if you're someone like me, who believes that a large component of success is good communication, then you're in the right place. I built my career on my ability to interact and communicate with others, and what I've leaned is that no matter where you go, people are people. Whether they're criminals or colleagues, the same principles apply: they're human and have mannerisms and gestures that can be suggestive of what they're thinking. If you're able to correctly interpret that information, you can use it to build stronger personal and professional relationships, which will ultimately lead to greater levels of success.

From suspects to businesspeople, from drug dealers to reputable citizens—I've dealt with them all. And I've always been able to find common ground in order to open lines of communication. By the time we get through discussing the different lessons I've learned, both in the academy and on the streets, you'll not only have an entirely new perspective on other people, but you'll also have one on your abilities and what you're truly capable of accomplishing. This will allow you to push beyond your own mental boundaries and reach your full potential. In each chapter, I'll encourage you to improve by constantly challenging yourself and those around you. I expect you to notice more, interpret better, and have a heightened awareness of opportunities relating to self-improvement. I want you to feel transformed.

Think of this book as a guided tour of the major lessons I learned in law enforcement, but don't worry; you're not going to have to wear a bulletproof vest and two chrome pistols like Will Smith in *Bad Boys*—although deep down, I know you might want to. All you have to do is begin each chapter with an open mind. I'll be there as we progress to explain exactly what I learned, how I used it to my advantage, and how you can apply it in your own life.

Most people are never exposed to this information. No matter how many police television shows you watch, or how many detective stories you've read, you never really get a taste of the actual training that I'm going to share with you, because, frankly, it's not always exciting. What *is* exciting is implementing the knowledge you obtain during your training into your daily routine and seeing positive results. *That* never gets old.

The approach that I'm sharing with you is perfectly appropriate for anyone, regardless of your age, gender, or occupation. One of the main differences between you and an experienced detective is that they've been trained to be more alert and to notice the little details that the average person doesn't take the time to pay attention to. I'll explain not only what to specifically look for, but also why it's important to pick up on these indicators. It's amazing what you can figure out about a person just through observing a subtle gesture.

When I was working undercover and unable to go out in public, I would watch *Big Brother*. The social aspect of the game reminded me a lot of my job. I would sit there with my wife and make comments like, "If I were on this show, I'd win." She'd laugh and reply with a simple "Okay." It sounds funny, right? There I am sitting in my living room, saying I'd win one of the most popular reality shows on television, and I'm sure I wasn't the only person out there saying that. But I had a different reason for wanting to be on the show than most. The things I learned during my years as a detective allowed me to develop a *hybrid* approach to dealing with people in all aspects of my life. I had combined my own interpersonal skills with years of law-enforcement training. As a result, I believed that the way I interacted with others would enable me to be a real contender in the game. I wanted to prove to myself that I was right.

The premise of the show is a contest between personalities, which entails trying to understand your competitors by anticipating their next move and redirecting them in a way that benefits *you*. This is essentially what we would do in the interrogation room with a suspect. Obtain a statement, dissect their behavior, and then use that information to get what we need. *Big Brother* involved individuals looking to win a game, not criminals attempting to avoid apprehension. But just like criminals, these players would be on high alert because of the setting and what was at stake. This would naturally make my job harder, but that's what I wanted. I had a unique approach to dealing with people regardless of the situation, and *Big Brother* was the chance to prove it. This was an opportunity for me to be placed in a controlled environment and to really test my theory out in front of seven million people.

Now you understand why I applied to be on the show. It wasn't merely because the program offered a half-million-dollar prize. Sure, I was interested in the cash so I could provide a better life for my wife and daughter, but it was more than that—much more. This was a chance to excel in a controlled social experiment and prove that no matter what the situation or the person I was dealing with, my approach was effective. If I could pull it off under those conditions, I could do it anywhere. Better yet, so can you.

I take pride in the fact that I was never voted out of that house and that I eventually won $575,000. I found common interests with all of my competitors. They trusted me, and I grew to understand them as individuals, which allowed me to anticipate their next move. My approach to communication and the ability to adapt ultimately resulted in my not only winning the game, but also being the first person in sixteen seasons to win without ever being nominated to leave the house.

This success is the clearest indication I can give you that my approach, which involves observation, communication, and adaptation, can help you in all facets of your life. My win on *Big Brother* was put on display for millions to see, clearly demonstrating that undercover skills—the same ones I'll teach you in this book—can enable you to have a better understanding of yourself and those around you. And make no mistake about it, I'm not writing this book because I won the show. I won the show because of what's in this book. Now you can take what I've learned and apply the same approach so *you* can come out a winner.

So where do we begin? The same way I started my career as a rookie officer in the police academy: by building a strong foundation.

You have to know the basics before we can get into the high-level stuff, and that involves figuring out who you are. You'll learn how to interact with people by taking advantage of your strengths and minimizing your weaknesses. I'll show you how to improve your natural attributes through practice and repetition, how to incorporate mental rehearsal into your daily preparation, and how to be an effective communicator both at work and during personal encounters.

Along the way, you're going to learn a lot about yourself and the people in your life. While absorbing all this information, take it seriously, but have fun with it. You've survived up to this point in your life, and whether you read this book or not, you'll continue to do so. Look at this for exactly what it is: an opportunity to grow and improve who you are as a person. After all, that's what you're trying to do, isn't it?

Do you want to be successful at work? Become a more capable leader? Develop stronger relationships with family and friends? Grow your abilities as a communicator? If you answered *Yes* to any of those questions, then you *should* get excited about what you're going to learn. The information in this book will help in those areas and many others, the same way it helped me. But from this point forward, it's not about *me* anymore. Now it's time for *you* to take advantage of the undercover edge.

CHAPTER ONE

||||||||||||||||||||||||||||||||||||||||||||||||||||||

DEFINE YOURSELF

"Holy shit! How was the high school prom, bud?"

I laughed a little, shook my head, and said, "Oh, boy, here we go."

"Bro, you look like you're twelve. How old are you?"

"I'm twenty."

"Jeez! I'm old enough to be your father."

There was an awkward silence for a second, and then I looked at him and smiled. "Does that mean I should start calling you Daddy?"

And that, ladies and gentleman, is how I started my first day at the police academy.

Not exactly how I had envisioned it, but it got a good laugh out of my classmates, and it definitely broke the ice. I didn't take any offense to my classmate's comments. I knew he wasn't being malicious. He was feeling the same emotions I was: anxiousness, curiosity, and excitement. His decision to bust my chops was more of a conversation starter and less of a knock on me. Before our brief interaction, no one had said a word, but after that exchange, we were more relaxed. We introduced ourselves and engaged in some small talk before we reached the entrance door of the academy. Together we entered the two-story building, knowing this was the start of the career that we had all worked so hard for.

Our class was very diverse. There were men, women, people of different backgrounds, and a wide range of ages. Although we were all different, we still shared many similarities. Most of us came from middle-class families. My dad, for example, was a stockroom manager at Brown University, and my mother worked for the school department. I had a younger brother and two younger sisters, and we had all grown up in Central Falls, Rhode Island. Both of my parents worked extremely hard to provide for us, and while we never went without, we certainly weren't rich either.

I really can't tell you why, but I felt comfortable with most of my classmates right from the start. We had an instant bond. We all knew what we were about to go through and that it wouldn't be easy. There was a high probability that a good percentage of us wouldn't make it. This wasn't the type of test where as long as you tried your hardest, you passed. There are no participation trophies in the police academy. They have strict guidelines and requirements that have to be met, and if you don't meet them, you're gone. It was obvious that we would need to rely on each other to make it to the end. Regardless of who we were or how we felt before entering the academy, we all had one thing in common: we wanted to graduate…and *that* was enough for all of us.

You might be wondering why I'm telling you all of this. What does it have to do with defining who you are as a person? I was very young when I entered the academy, and as much as I hate to admit it, I still had some growing up to do. Yes, I was mature for my age, but I didn't have the life experiences that most people accumulate by the time they become a police officer. I had only graduated college a few months earlier, and knowing how to do a keg stand doesn't exactly qualify you to carry a gun. I had to redefine who I was.

The academy jump-started my growing-up phase earlier than it would've occurred naturally. When you realize the severity of your responsibilities, it forces you to look in the mirror and ask yourself, "Can I really do this?" Sure, I knew being a police officer wouldn't be easy, but my vision of what it actually entailed came from movies like *Training Day* and *Speed*. It wasn't until I found myself sitting in class listening to stories from former police officers that I understood what the job really entailed. After reluctantly admitting to myself that I needed to mature as a person, I decided to make some changes in my life. Knowing that self-awareness was the key to self-improvement, I not only had to be more accountable for my actions, I also had to figure out how my mind was wired.

Would I be able to handle the stressors associated with this line of work? Understanding what I was mentally capable of dealing with would allow me to define who I currently was and who I needed to become in order to perform my duties. The quickest way to improve who you are is by understanding your abilities. If your goal is to become a better quarterback for your football team, how can you determine what areas you need to work on if you've never thrown a football? The same principle applies to improving your individual characteristics. You have to know your positive and negative qualities before you can begin to achieve personal growth.

Before I was hired by the Central Falls Police Department, I took a battery of psychological tests that we refer to as psych screening. While not as in-depth as psychoanalysis, psych screening can allow the applicant to determine some basic aspects of their personality. Sometimes the applicant gets nervous because they mistakenly fear that a psychologist will be able to peer into their unconscious and see their innermost thoughts. This isn't the case at all. The main purpose of the tests is to screen out people who might be unfit to work with other officers and the public.

Psych screening consists of two parts: the timed portion with a pen and paper and a clinical interview with an actual psychologist. Although the whole process sounds elaborate, you can do the same type of psych screening on yourself with a little thought and without having to take a written test or meet with a doctor. Conducting your own psychological screening will put you one step closer to defining who you are.

I'll outline two easy steps that you can take to perform a self-analysis, or psych screening, on yourself. The first step consists of analyzing your strengths, specifically those aspects of your personality that set you apart from other people. This part of your personal evaluation is pretty easy, since you're essentially patting yourself on the back, something most of us, including myself, have no problem doing.

The second step is recognizing your weaknesses and embracing them. This will enable you to isolate areas of yourself that you need to work on. Once you identify the areas that need improvement, you can develop exercises or implement changes in your behavior that will assist you in strengthening your vulnerabilities.

There are many techniques you can use to identify your strengths and weaknesses as well as to better understand your relationship with yourself and others. One of easiest and most effective tools is the Johari Window, which I'll explain in more detail later in the chapter.

After identifying your weaknesses and developing a strategy to improve them, what's next? The best way to determine whether your game plan for self-improvement is working is to establish goals and keep a record of your progression.

By having a phone or notebook on hand, you not only have the ability to write down your goals, but you might actually capture creative insights that increase your probability of accomplishing them. Regardless of what method you choose, adding new goals, updating old ones, and monitoring your progress is a valuable practice that you should get in the habit of doing.

YOUR PERSONAL TOOL KIT

Imagine that you're at a construction site and you're carrying around your toolbox. The problem is, you're not allowed to open it, and no one has told you what's inside. If you find yourself in this situation, it's going to be extremely difficult, if not impossible, for you to know what you're capable of accomplishing. But if you had the opportunity to look inside that toolbox, you'd have an entirely new perspective on what you could do. You would not only see what tools were available but also their quality and current condition, allowing you to choose the best tool for the job. So which situation would *you* prefer? Going in blind or being well prepared? Clearly the worker who can see what they have to work with is going to be in a better position to get the job done.

This tool-kit analogy holds true for each and every one of us in life. By taking a second to assess your situation objectively, you're going to be able to move forward knowing what you personally bring to the table and how to maximize your assets.

I want to take a second and emphasize that this is probably the most important chapter in the book, because this is when we figure out what's in *your* toolbox. Before we can move forward, we need to figure out what tools *you* possess. I'm going to show you how to recognize exactly what you're capable of—and what might be more challenging for you. Before you can learn how to deal with everyone else, you have to know yourself. Having a strong understanding of who you are will enable you to excel when dealing with others.

You'll see later in this book that the way you analyze yourself is the same way you analyze other people. By sizing someone up before interacting with them, you'll manage them more efficiently by prioritizing their strongest assets and utilizing them accordingly. The same idea applies when evaluating your own abilities. You might be a good speaker but a terrible listener. Or you might have an ability to read people accurately but an inability to effectively direct them. Whatever your situation is, being self-aware will allow you to deploy your personal assets appropriately.

DISCOVER YOUR OWN SUPERPOWERS

Some people refer to police officers as heroes. Obviously I'm a little biased, but I agree with that sentiment. They're out there trying to help others, and they risk their lives doing it.

Maybe that's the reason I like superheroes so much. As a kid, I enjoyed collecting comics, and with all the movies coming out over the last few years, my admiration for these fictional characters has only increased. I like them all: Superman, Batman, Iron Man, Spider-Man, Captain America, and the Hulk. I could name more but to avoid further embarrassment, I'll stop there.

They all possess different abilities that I admire, but if I could only pick one, I'd have to choose Superman. I always liked the fact that he could fly, bend steel with his bare hands, and stay cool under pressure. But just like anybody else, he had to learn what his superpowers were and how to use them. In fact, he had to discover his powers and abilities through trial and error. As he figured out what he could actually do, he developed a higher level of confidence in himself. And in every subsequent story, he would find a way to use his strengths to defeat the enemy.

In contrast, Spider-Man isn't as strong as Superman, but he's more agile and can climb buildings. He has the same goals as Superman—fighting crime and helping humanity—but he doesn't possess the same abilities. Instead, he uses his unique strengths, including his ability to spin webs and swing from building to building, to beat the bad guy.

The point I'm trying to make is that although Superman and Spider-Man have the same goals and want similar outcomes, they have two completely different approaches. They each use what *they're* good at to accomplish their mission. Spider-Man doesn't try to fly or lift up buildings; he stays within his limits and ultimately achieves the same result as Superman.

The way I see it, we all have superpowers. Almost everyone has one or more strengths, and once you figure out what *yours* are, you can begin to assess exactly how to utilize them effectively. We may have the same task, but the way we go about completing it will depend on our own individual attributes. If you're a good communicator who speaks well but not such a great writer, then focus on speaking to convey your message. If, on the other hand, you're a great writer but not the best speaker, focus on writing a self-explanatory speech and reduce the need for improvisation. There is no predetermined set of skills needed in order to be successful. It's not written anywhere that if you can't do certain things, you're destined for failure. What I'm telling you is that instead of trying to be someone else, figure out what works for *you* and use that knowledge to your benefit.

I've seen many police officers who want to become undercover detectives. And although they may have a passion for that line of work, it doesn't always pan out. Working in an undercover capacity requires certain qualities, and unfortunately, not all of them can be taught. It may not be easy to swallow this realization, but when officers focus on what they *can* do well, whether it's traffic enforcement or community policing, that's when they start to excel. Figuring out how to advance their career through the skills they *do* possess will lead to positive results. This doesn't mean that you can't still use the skills that aren't necessarily your best, but by prioritizing your top attributes, you're going to produce better work.

Regardless of your career choice—teacher, sales clerk, mechanic, or scientist—this philosophy applies to everyone. If you find yourself in an environment where advancement has become a struggle, you have to step back and reevaluate the situation. Maybe you're going about it all wrong. Ask yourself, "What position do I want to be in a year from now?" Then ask, "What are the possible paths I can take to get there?" If you find yourself with multiple answers to the second question, then the only thing left to figure out is which of the ways you have already tried. If you answer honestly, I can almost guarantee that most of you have only tried *one* avenue, and that's okay. We all get tunnel vision sometimes. But now that you've tried one way, it's probably a good idea to figure out an alternative. You've already spent so much time trying to compete with others in ways that may not be your strong point. What do you have to lose by trying another option? You may find that not only do you get to where you want to be, but you also possess a talent you didn't realize you had.

It's possible that you might be looking at the example above and assuming that it only applies to your professional life. But think about it for a second. You've probably witnessed or even implemented this approach in your life already. Have you ever had a romantic interest but had trouble gaining their attention? You think to yourself, "Man, all the guys she dates are athletes, but I'm not." And for some strange reason, even though you know it isn't your thing, you try to impress her by signing up for the football team. When it doesn't work out because, well, you're terrible, you become discouraged. Then you think about the situation and decide to take another shot. This time you ask her to attend an art exhibit, which is not only something you enjoy, but a topic you actually comprehend. She says "Yes," you go out, you're able to impress her with your knowledge, and you go on to live happily ever after...or something like that.

The point to the story is that the guy can still get the girl, but first he has to figure out what the best approach is for *him* and not rely on what everyone else is doing. Stay within yourself; figure out what *you're* good at; and the chances of you reaching your goals (regardless of what or who they are) will increase exponentially.

FACE THE FACTS

If you already know what you excel at, you're ahead of the game. But what if you haven't figured that out yet? We all have aspects of our personality that we don't know about. Carl Jung, a Swiss psychiatrist and psychotherapist, refers to these unknown aspects as our "Shadow." These unknown portions of ourselves could be strengths, or they could be weaknesses. That's for you to figure out.[1]

If everyone is telling you that you're a good leader, maybe there's some truth to it. Conversely, if everyone is telling you that you're a micromanager, perhaps there's some truth to that as well. I fully understand that we don't relish looking our negatives in the face; instead, we deny them, defend against them, or ignore them altogether. By confronting our shortcomings, we can usually gain at least some measure of control over them, and more often than not we can make significant improvements. It may be more difficult to see the negatives that people try to bring to your attention, but it's a necessary evil. And even when someone points out a specific flaw that they've recognized, you still may not believe or accept it for one reason or another. That's why it's important to discover these things for yourself. But how do you do it?

There is a psychological tool that can help you get more in touch with your undiscovered traits, both the positives and the more difficult-to-see negatives. As I mentioned at the beginning of this chapter, it's called the Johari Window.[2] Psychologists Joseph Luft and Harrington Ingham developed this model in 1955; the tool's name derived from a combination of their first names, Joe and Harry: "Joe-Harry" Window. I learned about the model during a psychology course in college and found the results to be dead-on in certain areas and eye-opening in others. Although simplistic, it was a very effective tool that anyone can benefit from. At a minimum, it will give you a visual of your personal characteristics, and sometimes we need to physically see something before we believe it.

JOHARI WINDOW

	Known to self	Not known to self
Known to others	**Arena**	**Blind spot**
Not known to others	**Façade**	**Unknown**

The four boxes represent aspects of the Self. Beginning in the upper left-hand corner, and moving clockwise, you start with the **Arena**, which corresponds to those aspects of the Self that are known to you *and* to others. For example, if you're a fast runner and have won a few races, then your running ability is known to you and to everyone else.

Next is the **Blind Spot**, which corresponds to aspects of the Self that are known to others but *unknown* to you. For example, you might be a bad listener without even knowing it, but other people might perceive this trait and may even be turned off by it, causing them to not communicate with you.

The third box, the **Unknown** quadrant, represents personal aspects that neither you nor others know. You might not know that you have a gift for writing poetry, and because you're not aware of it, you haven't written anything yet. And until you write something, no one else will know of your talent either.

The final quadrant, **Façade**, corresponds to aspects of the Self that are known to you but kept hidden from others. No, I'm not talking about your guilty pleasures. I'm referring to a passion or skill that the people in your life are unaware of. It may be that you enjoy classical music but only listen to it when you are alone, or that you like to paint in your free time but have never shown anyone your work.

I know you might be sitting there asking yourself, "How can I fill out areas about myself that I'm not even aware of yet?" This has a two-part answer. First off, you can't. The point of having these two areas as part of your self-analysis is a way of acknowledging that they exist, even if you don't know what they are. There are always going to be characteristics of your personal makeup that you don't know about yet; however, having an aspect of your personality in the unknown category doesn't mean it will be there a year or even a week from now. Understanding that you are constantly learning about yourself allows you to adapt to new revelations involving your abilities. In reality, you'll never fill out the Blind Spot or Unknown quadrants because once you become aware of a trait, it no longer qualifies for those categories. There are rare opportunities to "move" personal characteristics from the Blind Spot and Unknown areas to the Arena and Façade quadrants, which is why it's so important to listen to those around you. If you're receptive to feedback, something in their words may serve as an indicator for a possible character trait that you are currently unaware of. So pay attention; you may just learn something about yourself.

The value of the Johari Window depends upon your willingness to expand your understanding of who you are. If you're open-minded and willing to learn, then theoretically you can significantly shrink the size of your Blind Spot while simultaneously enlarging the size of your Arena. It's an opportunity to learn more about your abilities, and regardless of your findings, that's always a good thing. The better you know yourself, the quicker you can improve.

IDENTIFY YOUR WEAKNESSES AND EMBRACE THEM

So you've identified some weaknesses in your mental or physical abilities… Congratulations, you're human. We all have downfalls; they are part of who we are. But taking ownership of those weaknesses is the key to overcoming your limitations. Obviously, I'm not suggesting that you sit there and dwell on what you can't do. Doing so would only reinforce the existence of your limits, making them a bigger issue than they already are. But it does pay to know your deficiencies. This way you can avoid them before they trip you up, or at least relegate them to a secondary position until you can work through them.

It's our nature to deny weaknesses, defend against them, or even make excuses for them. Denying they exist will only hinder your long-term growth. Defending yourself is a waste of time, since it does nothing to alleviate the actual issue. And making excuses won't help you improve the attributes you're deficient in. It's always been my belief that the best course of action is to embrace your downfalls and face them head-on.

For instance, if you work in a hotel kitchen and you know you're a good cook but a poor speaker, it's probably in your best interest to become a chef rather than a maître d'. When you accept responsibility and acknowledge your shortcomings—in this case your inability to interact with people—you can take steps to improve. Start slow and begin by talking more with the kitchen staff. Then venture out and speak with a few tables about your food. As time passes, you'll naturally become more comfortable, which will also increase your ability to speak in front of larger groups. Again, you may never be the person who's going to hop up on stage during dinner, but that doesn't mean you can't increase your social skills to an acceptable level. Knowing where you struggle and making a conscious effort to continuously work on those areas is the key to your progression.

It's never a good thing to be one-dimensional, a saying we hear all too often in sports and in business. It's always advantageous to be well rounded, regardless of what arena you're looking to excel in. Whether it's at work or in your personal life, being versatile allows you to build relationships with a variety of people because of your ability to adapt to any situation.

When I was in high school, I played basketball. I wasn't the best player on the team, but I was decent. I was known for my shooting ability, but the big knock on my game was my inability to dribble the ball with my left hand. I'm right-handed, so naturally I always felt more comfortable dribbling with that hand. The problem was that the opposing teams started to notice this flaw and began shading the defense to my right, forcing me to either dribble with my left or pass the ball. I usually chose the latter. That summer, I decided to improve my skills. I would take my basketball everywhere I went but would only dribble with my left hand. Even during pickup games, I would force myself to go to my left. For a while, it wasn't pretty but I got better. I started to feel more comfortable, and it became more natural. The next season I was a better player, because I was more versatile. Yes, my right hand was still my go-to, but if I needed to rely on my left-handed dribbling to get to the hoop, I was able to do so.

When I attended the police academy, I learned a lot about my physical capabilities through the training we underwent. We covered everything, including shooting accuracy on the firing range, speed on the track, and strength and agility during ground fighting classes. I loved it all, but I wasn't perfect at everything—nobody was. I was pretty good at ground fighting but less than stellar at running. To be honest, running has never really been my thing. When it comes to long-distance running I'm okay, but I'm never going to win any track meets.

Knowing these things about myself never hindered my ability as a police officer. In fact, it had just the opposite effect. If I ever felt that I was going to end up in a fight on the ground with a suspect, I was confident that I could handle the situation or at least hold my own until backup arrived. However, if I was dealing with an individual who I knew had been in foot pursuits in the past, I would immediately let the officers in the area know the situation before he even took off. Why? It's tough to admit, but if he had decided to go for it, I wasn't confident I could catch him. Between the twenty-pound belt and my ability (or lack thereof) to run, the odds were not in my favor. But I knew this about myself, accepted it, and didn't let my ego get in the way. I didn't wait until he bolted before losing him over a fence. I approached the situation with an understanding of my abilities and the knowledge of how to avoid being defeated due to my own deficiency.

And before you say, "Well, it must be embarrassing to have to call for help from your buddies," let me tell you, as a police officer it's *much* more embarrassing to have someone take off on you and lose them in the first two minutes. Trust me, I've been there before, and it's a lesson you only need to learn once. The guys at the department have a way of making sure you don't forget about it, and it usually involves your face, photoshopped on an unflattering body in a compromising position, with a witty one-liner written across the top of it. And it's not just one copy; that's too easy—they're plastered all over the station for everyone's enjoyment.

Remember, being truthful with yourself is critically important. It's relatively easy to discern your strengths but significantly harder to accept your shortcomings. Check your ego at the door and do some soul searching. Once you identify your weaknesses, own them. No one's perfect. You're better off figuring out your flaws now and making the necessary adjustments, as opposed to denying they exist and having them bite you in the ass later.

WHO DO YOU WANT TO BE?

We've talked a lot about knowing your strengths and weaknesses, because it lets you know where you are *right now*. But that's only where you are *today*, and there's nothing stopping you from making changes. Assessing yourself—both your positives and negatives—is the prerequisite for moving forward. You can decide to become a better speaker, a more sensitive listener, or a stronger leader. It's up to you where you go next.

After you finish your own self-evaluation, the next step should be to set goals that increase your abilities. In school, you can set up educational goals. At work, you can design business goals. And for self-improvement, you can create personal goals. They can be daily, weekly, monthly, or even yearly, and they should all have one purpose: to create a better version of yourself. It can be something as simple as attending a weekly class in order to learn a new language before your trip to Spain in three months. It could also be a long-term goal that will involve multiple components, such as learning to be a better leader by attending trainings, adjusting your delivery at work, and developing better relationships with your subordinates.

Once you decide what you need to improve, you take it on through incremental steps. You can't go from 0 to 100 in one day. You have to figure out all intricacies of the overall mission and break them down into smaller, more obtainable goals. This not only results in a more efficient process, it gives you small victories along the way, which will serve as motivation to continue. As you progress, you'll become a different person, creating a sense of accomplishment and a feeling of fulfillment. Moving forward in this manner will lead to a constant evolution of who you are.

So you're sitting there saying, "Okay, Derrick, I'll buy it. But how do I keep track of all these goals that I want to accomplish?

How do I hold myself accountable?" I'm a visual person. I always learn better by seeing what I need to do, so being able to physically review my goals keeps me on track. When I'm at work, I always have a notebook and pen with me. It's a major convenience to have the ability to record something as soon as you learn of it. There have been times where I'm investigating five cases at once, so when it comes to remembering names, addresses, and times, I have to write it all down. However, I'm all about technology, so for my personal goals and business ventures outside of the police department, my note-taking goes digital. If we have an opportunity to be more efficient by utilizing new tech, we should capitalize on it. I'm a gadget guy: iPhone, iPad, Apple Watch, MacBook—I'm into all of it. I do some of my best thinking when I'm at the gym or in the shower, so when I have an idea, I immediately stop what I'm doing and punch it into my phone. I type notes, reminders, inspiring quotes, whatever I want. But more than anything else, I use my phone to set up goals and track my progress. It's quick, convenient, and always accessible. If you saw my phone right now, you would see a list of daily, weekly, and monthly reminders that I use to keep myself focused. But the truth is, there isn't just one right answer. Everyone is different.

Some people prefer to buy a dry-erase board and stick it on a wall or refrigerator. That's fine, but for me, I'm not too fond of everyone seeing what I'm trying to do. I would prefer to have someone point out the difference they see in my strengths without knowing that I've been actively improving them. This is also a way of confirming that the positive feedback you're receiving is genuine.

Other people choose to keep everything in their head. If you can do that, more power to you, but for me that would become confusing. Deciding to do everything in your head also makes it easier to neglect certain goals, because you can't set reminders or monitor your progress.

We have a saying in law enforcement: "If you didn't write it down, it didn't happen." I try to maintain that mind-set when it comes to goal planning and documenting my progress. It's also motivating to see intangible ideas materialize into reality. Sometimes I look back at the goals I had set for myself a year ago to see how far I've come since then. It's gratifying to see what you've already achieved, and it can even give you a boost of motivation if you hit a plateau during your transformation.

Keep in mind that you can change your goals as you progress. You can keep them current by modifying them slightly, crossing things off that you've already completed, and adding new variables to make them more specific to what you want to accomplish.

Defining yourself on paper is a way of visually seeing who you are today and who you want to be tomorrow. In between these past and future selves are the goals you need to complete in order to bridge that gap. Tracking your objectives and capturing milestones during your progress is what gives you the motivation to keep pushing forward. Take your time and put some thought into how you want to tackle your goals. Really visualize yourself carrying out each step as you write them down. Believe that they're not just words on a piece of paper; they're actions that you *will* fulfill. And don't be afraid to aim high when it comes to envisioning the person you aspire to be.

It's pretty simple. The only thing stopping you from developing into the best version of yourself is you. Emphasize your strengths, minimize your weaknesses, know where you want to be, and design a plan to get you there. *That's* the winning formula for defining not only who you are now, but who you will become.

CHAPTER TWO

||||||||||||||||||||||||||||||||||||||||||||||||||||||||||||

KNOW YOUR TARGET

In my line of work, when we're conducting surveillance on a suspect, we usually refer to them as the "target" of the investigation. And while monitoring the target, we attempt to learn as much as we can about that person.

Who do they hang out with? What's their favorite place to eat? Where do they work out? What time do they wake up, and what time do they go to sleep?

These are just a few of the questions we try to answer, but nothing is off limits. Everyone has a pattern, and you can learn a lot about someone just by observing their routine for a few days. The goal is to develop a complete profile on the target so we can tailor our investigation around who they are and what makes them tick, allowing us to anticipate their next move.

Let me first assure you that my approach to reading people is just as valid in business and personal relationships as it is in police investigations and undercover work. The major difference is that in *your* world you won't be using your observations to make a decision about whether you should arrest someone or utilize them as a confidential informant. The severity of your conclusions doesn't always have to be that dramatic. It's more likely that you'll find these techniques useful when deciding whether or not to trust someone in a business deal, asking a romantic interest on a date, building on an existing relationship with a family member or friend, or determining the true intentions of a complete stranger. Regardless of the application, being able to read people accurately will allow you to approach them in a way that they'll be more receptive to.

Coming from my personal and professional background, I get a pretty good read on most people fairly quickly. But I didn't learn this skill set overnight. Likewise, I can't promise that you'll be able to do everything I can do right away. Growing up and having to deal with some tough situations, I found myself needing to be constantly aware of my surroundings and the people in them. As a detective, I worked in many life-or-death scenarios, and my ability to decipher who the bad guys were was extremely important. It takes time, but I'm going to share these skills with you, so that eventually you'll be able to use the same observational techniques to discover the truth about the people in your life.

BUILD A PROFILE

Let's say you're planning to have lunch with someone new, maybe a friend of a friend. Before you even meet this new person, it might be a good idea to start thinking about them in the same manner that I think about the people I'm investigating. I refer to this as "building a profile," and doing so allows you to develop a preliminary background on the person before even meeting them. It may be information pertaining to work, marriage, children, and anything else that you should be aware of before interacting with them:

"Hey, just so you know, this guy is going through an ugly divorce. So stay away from the family conversation."

"They are very religious, so don't use profanity."

I'm sure most of you have already had conversations like this in the past, but this is still a form of intelligence gathering. The truth is that detectives don't have some secret list of questions we attempt to answer during a surveillance operation. The information you gather before meeting new people is the same type of information we collect about the target of a criminal investigation. And don't let the word *target* scare you off. This is just a technical term that we're using to describe anyone or anything we want to become more familiar with—*not* a military mind-set we're looking to implement. Essentially, you could be referring to an individual you just met, so there are no negatives associated with calling someone a target in the way that we're doing here. (However, I wouldn't suggest using the term to their face. We'll keep that one between us.)

All that said, the term *target* is in fact very appropriate, since it allows us to be objective in our thinking about a person or place. We don't want emotion to skew our judgment; we're looking for the facts. When you think objectively, you're able to make a more accurate assessment.

So how do we develop a profile on a target using the same mind-set detectives have during an undercover investigation? It all starts with being receptive to information that's already out there. For example, what are other people saying about your target? How do people talk about them when their name is mentioned? Are they considered to be erratic or stable? What are some of their likes and dislikes?

You may be wondering why we would care about what they like or dislike, and there's a simple explanation. If I'm going undercover and want the best chance of infiltrating the target's inner circle, I want to make sure it appears that we have numerous things in common, even if we don't. When it comes to your personal life, the same principles apply, and the best place to start is with your target's friends. Before being introduced to someone, a mutual friend might say something like, "She's really into photography," or "He enjoys golf." These offhand comments can help you build a profile on the person, so that when you finally meet them, you already have a few talking points.

If this person were a love interest, the questions would obviously be more personal. Are they single? Have they ever been married before? What hobbies do they enjoy? Do they have a good sense of humor? All these pieces of information go together to build up your understanding of the person and help you decide how to approach the situation appropriately. You can file away all of the intelligence you receive based on what you consider more or less important, which will ultimately depend on what you're attempting to do.

Most of the questions above would apply to building a stronger relationship with someone, but the term "target" doesn't only apply to people. If it were a business or a corporation where you were seeking employment, the questions would obviously be different. What does the company specialize in? Do they have a mission statement? What are their core values? Who is the CEO, and what is their background? What does the application process consist of? What type of people do they usually employ? These are the questions you would most likely start with before expanding your inquiry based on what your intelligence gathering revealed.

This brings up a crucial point: When building a profile, you have to remember that it's dynamic and will change based on what you're researching. There's no predetermined set of questions that will apply to every situation. Everyone and everything is different, even if it's only by a small margin. Start with the basics and let your investigation go wherever the answers take you.

Imagine you are applying to two sales companies. They seem very similar: they're the same size, they're in the same location, and they're selling the same product. You do your research on one of the two companies before interviewing and assume that the second business is so similar to the first one that there is no need to repeat the process. However, down the road you find out that the human resources manager at the company you did *not* investigate went to school with one of your best friends. Do you think that piece of information would have been helpful during the hiring process? Maybe, maybe not; but it wouldn't have hurt to have been aware of it.

And if you're saying, "Well, it's not fair to use that type of information to your advantage," my response is simple: If you're qualified for the job, you do whatever you can to get an edge on the competition, as long as it's ethically acceptable. Getting a little extra time during an interview because you're a "friend of a friend" is fair game in my book.

Even though I do it for a living, I still enjoy watching movies and television shows about cops and some of the work we do. Of course, not all depictions are created equal. Some are a stretch from how our job really works, but in most cases, when you see a detective searching for information about a suspect, we do employ a lot of the same practices and techniques. So don't be afraid to take a few pointers if you see something on television, especially with shows like *The First 48,* where the tactics depicted are pretty spot-on.

Detectives aren't the only ones who build profiles on people. A lot of successful salespeople, who take a large number of meetings and want to leave good impressions, keep notes about their clients. When they learn that one of them has a son named Harry who's going to medical school, they jot it down. A month later, when it's time to talk with that client again, they review their notes.

"Hey, how are you? How's your son Harry doing? Is he still enjoying med school?"

The client immediately feels more comfortable with the salesperson who remembered some trivial facts about their personal life. This builds a bond with the client and makes them feel as if the salesperson is not just there to sell a product.

It's easy to think, "The client will see right through this and know it's just a sales tactic." And you may be right, but how many pitches has that same client heard before this one where the salesperson didn't even *attempt* to build a personal rapport? If I have a bunch of people treating me like I'm just a number, and then one salesperson takes the time to ask me about my daughters, as long as everything else is on equal terms, who do you think I'm going to buy from?

The best salespeople know that they've got to keep things personal. By building their profiles on the people they sell to, they can maintain that important human connection, which extends outside the walls of the office. This doesn't only apply to clients; this is for everyone in the workplace. Keep mental or physical notes on the people you work with, including birthdays, names of spouses and kids, and any other important facts that you can think of. A simple phone call wishing a business associate a happy birthday can go a long way. Now, you may look at that as "ass-kissing," but I prefer to call it "networking."

Don't stop at the people you work with; take the same types of personal notes on friends and family. You might think this is an unusual thing to do. However, when you see the reaction you get from a fellow parent or your spouse's best friend when you not only remember their children's names, but also the names of their grandchildren, you'll understand what I'm talking about. Don't believe me? Take a second and consider all of your friends who have grandchildren, and think about how many of their names you actually know. If I were to guess, I'd say not many, and that's okay—it's usually not expected. *That's* what makes knowing that type of information about a person so impressive.

One more comment about note-taking and building a personal profile on someone: it's always best to do so without your target knowing. Most of you have probably seen a police officer taking notes at a crime scene, and I'm not saying that's wrong. It's okay to write things down when you're taking in a lot of detailed information, but don't have your head in a notebook the entire time. You don't know how many times I've had to tell a rookie to put their pen and paper away while they're talking to someone who has just been robbed. Engage with the person, and if you're actually listening to what they're saying, you'll remember the majority of the conversation and record what you need when it's over.

The other advantage to discreetly building a profile on someone is that when you do catch them off guard by mentioning an unfamiliar fact about them or their family, it will have much more of a lasting impact. Adversely, if the person feels that your comments are scripted or disingenuous, it could have a negative effect on the overall conversation. I have friends who write down their wedding anniversary so they don't forget the date. But when they give their wife a present, they don't say, "Honey, I saw on the calendar that it's our anniversary, so here's your present." That would only lead to a lonely night on the couch. Moral of the story: keep your notes to yourself. They're there to make you look better, not worse.

FEEDBACK IS YOUR FRIEND

I occasionally use a bit of psychology on the job and in my dealings with certain characters in my off time. One of the things I've come to appreciate is that all human beings are different, and one of the most meaningful ways we differ is in our openness to experience. Some individuals are open-minded and eager to learn new things. They're like sponges, absorbing new data and seeing what the other people, those who are more close-minded, don't care to notice.

When I'm trying to solve a crime, I will invariably encounter people who are able to absorb everything that's going on around them, whereas others are oblivious to what's happening right in front of their face. This distinction is obviously a spectrum, with the people who are receptive to different viewpoints at one end, and those set in their ways on the other. But I consider this diversity an important aspect of humanity, because while it's possible to perceive your actions and the behavior of others differently from your peers, the willingness to listen to different perspectives is essential to receiving feedback.

Have you ever walked away from a conversation with multiple people and said, "Wow, they were being an ass"? But another person disagrees, saying something like, "I didn't think so! It seemed like they were just busting your chops." Although you both heard and saw the same conversation, you interpreted the interaction differently. Being receptive to both verbal and nonverbal interpersonal feedback will allow you to deal with almost any situation in a more effective manner and will also allow you to make adjustments to your own conduct if needed.

Not only are some of us more naturally capable of processing this type of feedback, but there are differences in how genders process information as well. As a general rule, women (sorry, guys) are better than men at noticing facial expressions and reading them for their emotional significance. Obviously there are exceptions, but this is my opinion as a self-proclaimed "mama's boy" and also as a husband whose wife is always in tune with the emotional state of our children. But even though some people are better than others at reading interpersonal feedback, what I'm emphasizing is that *everyone* can improve their ability to do so, and understanding someone's true feelings will help you to interact with them on a more personal level.

How can you improve your innate ability to read the emotional state of the people you encounter? Start by asking yourself questions like:

- How are they verbally responding to the way you're communicating with them? Is it positive or negative?
- Are they short with their answers, or do they take the time to express themselves?

- What type of tone are they using?
- What does their body language tell you? Do they seem interested in what you're talking about?

By keeping yourself alert to these kinds of questions, you're increasing your ability to receive and interpret feedback, particularly the feedback that people communicate with their tone of voice, mannerisms, and subtle eye movements. Keep in mind that the ability to interpret what someone *is* saying is important, but it's equally essential to figure out what they're *not* saying.

Don't be afraid to look a person directly in the eye when you're having a conversation with them. It's a way of showing respect and lets them know that you are paying attention and committed to the conversation. Additionally, listen to their statements and see if their mannerisms are consistent with what they're saying. You don't have to stare, but be alert to what their mouth *and* their eyes are telling you. Think about it for a second: you could be in a situation where someone pays you a compliment, but by the tone of their voice and their body language, you know it's not sincere. Deciphering what someone is *really* saying will help you adjust the way you communicate with them while you're still in the middle of the conversation.

This tactic is something I use all the time in an interrogation. If

I'm trying to build a rapport with someone before asking the tough questions, I start with some casual conversation. By looking at their eyes, listening to their responses, and observing their overall body language, I can see what grabs their attention and what loses it. If I find that a particular topic has caused them to relax and become more comfortable with me, I'll continue with that conversation until I feel they're ready to answer what I really want to know.

Being observant has benefited me in multiple situations, not just police work. Opportunities to better understand those around you present themselves all the time if you know what to look for. How often have you heard a friend say, "I had *no idea!*" when they learn new information about someone they are supposedly close to? The question is, was the person being particularly secretive or did your friend have their blinders on?

If a person is acting noncommunicative or sullen, be alert that there might be something bothering them, something that they're not telling you. Sometimes all it takes is a few questions to elicit the information you're looking for.

"Is something wrong? Is there something you'd like to talk about? I can see that you're upset. What is it?"

Questions like these, asked at the appropriate time, can often lead to crucial revelations and discoveries. Don't get me wrong; you don't want to be forceful. You're taking a chance every time you ask questions of this nature, and even the best communicators have been guilty of making the right inquiry at the wrong time. However, taking these risks is part of the game of getting to know a person better, and a judicious use of nudging queries like these can often lead to a new line of communication. The more you try this approach, the better you'll get at it. So don't be too hard on yourself if you occasionally rub someone the wrong way with your inquisitiveness. The goal is to be more open to people and figure out where their heads are at. Unless you're a mind reader, the only way to do that is by asking questions.

Understanding feedback all boils down to empathy and the ability to walk in another's shoes. Either way, everyone who gives a genuine effort can make improvements in their ability to read the people they encounter. We developed this ability as human beings because it's a pivotal part of how we adapt and survive. In our society, it's vital that we understand our neighbors. This allows us to enter into commerce, build things together, and share and learn from each other's experiences. So if you find it challenging to read people and get feedback from their nonverbal communication, rest assured that it's a basic human skill, and know that you *can* do it. Just as with everything else in life, the more time you put into it, the more you'll get out of it.

UNDERSTANDING MOTIVATION

When you're trying to figure someone out, it's important to know their ambitions and what motivates them. I know that my *Big*

Brother fans will find this discussion particularly interesting, as it was a very important part of my strategy throughout the entire game. I used motivation to my advantage whenever possible. Believe it or not, understanding what motivates a person can play a big part in getting what you want out of them. The ability to recognize how to incentivize should be a prerequisite to any conversation where your intent is to elicit a specific response.

Using motivation as a tool is something that I enjoy discussing, because I utilize this technique almost every day in law enforcement as a supervisor. You have to accept that, in most cases, people need to feel that their actions are beneficial to them. It's amazing what a person will do when they're motivated. If it's something that they find valuable, something that they want to obtain, they will go to great lengths to reach it. But the real key is figuring out exactly what that motivating factor is.

Although motivation is a powerful tool, not everyone is influenced by the same factors. Some people are motivated by financial incentives. Others do their best work to receive verbal recognition or to increase their chances of being promoted. Then you have people who do things to impress a significant other or make family members proud.

Does it really matter *why* people are doing a good job, as long as they get the job done?

I don't think so.

One of the most important responsibilities we have as managers is putting our people in a position to succeed by identifying what motivates *them*.

Fully understanding motivation and the impact it has on performance is what enables a supervisor to influence the behavior of their team members.

In many ways, *Big Brother* represents a microcosm of our society and epitomizes the power of persuasion and influence. While I was on the show, I used motivation as my main tactic for getting individuals, whom I didn't know personally, to do what I needed them to do. I'm not going to name names, but there were people in that house who were there for reasons other than winning the game or the money. I quickly realized after a few conversations that some of them were primarily interested in fame, notoriety, and recognition. They wanted to use the show as a stepping-stone for an acting, modeling, or singing career. You have to discover these things by listening carefully to what people say, and also how they behave when they say it.

So how did I figure out the motivations of my competitors? I could see how excited some of them would get when they talked about the possibility of becoming famous. I laugh when I think about it now because it was all in good fun and for the sake of the game, but a few examples definitely stand out in my mind. I remember that certain contestants would constantly sing in the house and would even mention that they had applied for well-known singing shows in the past. It became very clear to me that they had aspirations of becoming a musician and in their minds, this was an opportunity to be "discovered." So when I needed something from that person, what did I say?

"Hey, man, if you do this [task that I wanted them to do], you got a good chance of winning the money." No, because I knew that although money was in the back of their mind, it wasn't their main focus. So instead, I would say to them:

"Hey, man, I'll tell you what. If you did this, it might catch the eye of some music producers or record labels."

"You think so, Derrick? You really think someone would notice?"

"Absolutely," I'd reply. "I think the fact that you're doing this is really going to capture the hearts of America and give you the exposure you need."

I motivated plenty of people to do things that probably weren't in the best interests of their overall *Big Brother* game…but they did it anyway, not knowing that what I was having them do was actually best for *my* game.

How does that relate to the business world? In any kind of company or corporation, there are going to be times as a manager when individuals in your group aren't motivated by the same things that motivate you. But in order to accomplish the overall goal, you need that person to want to do what you need them to do. So how do you accomplish that?

It all begins with knowing your people. For example, you may have a person who likes to catch their children's soccer games on Fridays, but unfortunately it starts at 3:00 p.m. and they don't get off work until 5:00 p.m. Well, maybe you say to them:

"Hey, listen. I need to have those Excel sheets done by two o'clock, and if you're able to get them done, I'll let you out of here by two-thirty so you can go to your kid's game."

Offer that proposition and then watch how quickly they kick into gear. You see, it might not seem like much to you, but it means a lot to them. So they're going to sit at their desk and they're not going to lift their head until those Excel sheets are done. And because they don't want you to have any problems with their work while they're gone, it's probably going to be done right the first time.

What if it's recognition or promotion that motivates them?

"Listen, Sue, I know this isn't what you wanted to do, but I need you to complete the assignment by Thursday. If you do that, I'm going to make sure that the bosses know that you really stepped up on this one. That'll give me the ammo I need to go to bat for you on the next project, and we can get you assigned to something that you really want to do."

Know your people. That's the key. Know them so well that you can motivate them at any time with just a few key words. Just make sure that you mean what you say and that you can deliver on any promises you make. Making false promises will only hurt your credibility and hinder your ability to motivate people in the future. But if you stay true to your word, people will be more inclined to follow your direction without questioning the reasoning behind it. Be honest with yourself and those you interact with. If you maintain that mind-set, persuasion and motivation will become some of the most valuable tools in your mental toolbox.

RECEIVING PRAISE

It's one thing to know what motivates a person; it's a whole different story to understand what type of recognition they're most receptive to receiving.

Whenever I work with a group of people on an assignment, at work or in a social setting, I keep in mind that people react differently to praise. Why is this on my radar? Praise and commendation are some of the chief motivating tools in making different types of people work together harmoniously. But one of the things that many leaders forget is that people respond to different forms of acknowledgment, and you can't count on a pat on the back or a thank-you to have the same effect on every person. When profiling someone, especially an employee or a significant other, it's important to understand his or her preference.

People sometimes make the fundamental mistake of assuming

that everyone receives praise the same way that they do. For example, *you* might like expensive gifts, but when you give someone else an expensive gift in order to impress them, it might not have the same effect. That doesn't necessarily mean it's not a nice gift. It may just be that the person doesn't value material possessions in the same way.

This philosophy is applicable in a variety of situations. Whether you're at work dealing with employees, completing a group project with some friends, or communicating with your kids, it's the same story, just different characters. But when I'm asked to give a specific example, I always go to the classic—husband and wife.

Yes, you can still develop a profile on your husband or wife. In all actuality, most of us already have. You may not have written them down, but you know your significant other's likes, dislikes, and everything in between. That said, sometimes our partners are a little out of touch with what we like. I think it's safe to say that most men find one form of praise preferable to all others, and that is…physical touch. I know. Shocker! But it's true. If you want to show your man you are pleased with something he's done, physical intimacy, which could be as simple as a kiss, usually works. However, when your husband is pleased with something you've done, he assumes that you respond to praise the same way. And although this may be the case in certain situations, it's probably not as often as he would like. You may just want some verbal recognition. A simple "Hey, thanks for everything you do" or "You look beautiful in that dress." Words can be powerful if they're sincere, and that may be all you're looking for from him. There also may be occasions when you're looking for a little more "praise"…let's say a new handbag, a piece of jewelry, or even an unexpected getaway.

I know the scenario above is probably familiar to you, even if you're not married. And although it's relatable, there's a point that many people miss. Regardless of how little or how well you know someone, part of developing a profile is realizing that there's a clear distinction between *what* they like and *when* they want it. It would serve you well to know the difference.

As we've seen in this chapter, clearly identifying who or what your target is will be one of the most important factors to accomplishing your goals. And it's not enough to just select a target; you need to learn everything you can about who they are and what they represent in order to develop a complete profile.

Taking notes on the people in your personal and professional life can assist in creating a deeper understanding of their motives. You can then use that knowledge in conjunction with the feedback you receive to determine the best way to interact with them.

The ability to read others can be enhanced with practice, and there's a lot of interesting information that can be extracted from vocal expressions and physical mannerisms. If you put all of this observational work together, you'll be able to build an approach specifically designed to elicit whatever response you're looking for. As an added benefit, knowing people on a personal level is not only satisfying, it makes you stand out from the crowd and leaves a lasting impression.

Whether your intention is to motivate an individual to perform a certain task or to entice a company to hire you for a specific job, understanding who your target is and what they're most receptive to will allow you to control the outcome.

CHAPTER THREE

||||||||||||||||||||||||||||||||||||||||||||||||||||||||

START AT HEADQUARTERS

I'm a practical-minded person, and I'm always looking for ways to simplify my life. I expect the things that I invest in to add value to my personal growth. If I eventually determine they're no longer contributing to my success, I eliminate them, but if they consistently improve my quality of life, I make them a priority. I have found that there are three main aspects of our lives that are extremely valuable when it comes to personal advancement and producing any kind of success: health, wealth, and family. These three components also happen to be pillars of the American Dream.

Most people today are seeking health, wealth, and a good family life, even though they may not see eye to eye on exactly how to achieve these three necessities. In this chapter, I'm going to outline what I've found to be an effective way to secure these foundational values.

The term *headquarters* should be viewed as a metaphor for our home life. For a cop, headquarters is the home base. It's where you can turn off the sensors for a few minutes and relax. I can tell you from experience that the way I conducted myself in the police station and the way I conducted myself out on the road were two completely different things. In the station, I was "Derrick." On the street, I was "Sergeant Levasseur." With the name change came a completely different personality. That same mentality applies when we're in our home surrounded by the people we trust.

Home is a place where you can take chances and get advice from the people who sincerely want to see you succeed. I don't think many would argue that there's no place we can let our guard down more than under our own roof. In that environment, we're allowed to be ourselves. It's the foundation of our lives, and if it's strong and supportive, our likelihood of reaching our full potential becomes a greater possibility. If you try to go out and accomplish your goals before making sure that the people you surround yourself with are solid, you may be in for a rough ride. But your home life is about more than friends and family; it's also about keeping your mind and body right and making sure that you're financially responsible. This is where the phrase "It starts at headquarters" comes into play, and I hope it's one that you embrace.

We'll talk a lot about your "home life" throughout this chapter. I put that phrase in quotation marks because it has a dual meaning. It's not only where you usually start your day, it's also what you build your success upon; however, it's important to remember that your house is only as strong as the foundation it's built on. If you half-ass the most important part of your home, it'll never be right, and there's only so much a coat of paint can hide. This also applies to life, and this is why health, wealth, and family should always be the three main components of *your* foundation.

YOU ONLY GET ONE

My grandmother used to tell me all the time, "Your health is the most important thing." When I was ten years old, I thought it was funny to hear her say that, but as I've grown older, I realize where she was coming from. She knew the value of health because as we age, we begin to break down, and there are some things in the body that you just can't fix. There's a saying: It's not like a car; you can't just trade it in. When it comes to your body, you only get one.

This is the cornerstone of my placing such a high value on health. Since we only get one body, if something goes wrong with it, we're going to be at a disadvantage. It makes sense to treat health as a core value, since it's necessary for almost everything we wish to do in life. Yes, it's true that you can have physical limitations and still accomplish your objectives. But, whenever possible,

49

one of our main responsibilities should always be to make sure we're running on all cylinders. It's going to be easier to achieve your goals if your body is at peak performance, not only because of the physical benefits, but also the mental benefits that accompany a healthy lifestyle.

EXERCISE

I go to the gym on a regular basis, and I've been doing so since I started the police academy. I did some weight training in college while playing baseball, but I wasn't consistent until my health became part of my job. No matter what your age, I highly recommend devoting time each day to exercise. Working out clears your mind by releasing endorphins into the body. Sometimes as people get older, they become apprehensive about going to a gym because they feel everyone is younger or in better shape. The truth is, there are many gyms where people in their fifties, sixties, and even older are still working out daily. On top of that, there are people in their twenties, thirties, and forties who are in no better shape than you might be. Instead of seeing age or your current appearance as a negative, think of it as a positive: you're an encouraging example of someone who's decided to actually do something about their health. Keep in mind that every day when you enter the gym, you're in better shape than the last time you left.

It's also true that being in shape physically can boost your mood. The connection between fitness and a positive mental attitude has been demonstrated in many studies, and doctors will often recommend exercising regularly to increase mental clarity.[3] Stress reduction is one of the by-products of going to the gym on a regular basis and a major reason it should be part of your normal routine.[4] Running, cycling, and other aerobic sports can enhance the way you feel, which allows you to think more clearly and make better decisions. How often do you find yourself in a situation where you're in a bad mood and say or do something that you later regret? Even though your words or actions can occur in the heat of the moment, they can have a lasting impact. They can ruin friendships, end romantic relationships, or undo the work you've put into creating your own personal profile. When I find myself in a bad place mentally, I usually jump right on social media to take my mind off things. What ends up happening is I see one negative comment and respond to it. Almost immediately, I regret it but it's too late at that point. I don't care how fast you delete it. Once you hit "send," the internet owns it, and a screenshot can immortalize almost anything. For that reason I now make a conscious effort to keep the phone out of my hands and substitute a quick run or a trip to the gym to let off some steam. More times than not, my urge to respond is gone by the time I get home.

Here's a little test I want you to try next time you're on

Facebook, Twitter, Instagram, or whatever platform you like to use. When you find a comment or post that you don't like and want to respond to…*don't*! Instead, put the phone down or step away from the computer, and take a walk around the block for ten minutes. During that time, you'll probably think about what you wanted to say. You'll even try out different versions of how you would've said it…but then something will happen. You'll think about the consequences. Not only are you starting an argument with the person who made the original comment or post, but now you also have to explain to everyone else why you responded in the first place. Then you'll find yourself wondering, *Is it really worth it?* In most cases the answer will be *No,* further proving that only a few minutes of physical stimulation can help you avoid a few days of regret.

SLEEP

Even though regular exercise can help in your decision-making process, it won't do much good if you're failing to get enough sleep. I'm not a doctor and by no means an expert on sleep, but as a guy who worked the graveyard shift for five years, I cannot emphasize enough how crucial rest is to an overall program of health and fitness.

I'm one of those people who needs nine hours of sleep to feel well rested. Anything less than that and the first part of my day is a struggle. With working the overnight shift and having a family at home who was awake during normal hours, I found myself cutting down on the amount of time I slept so that I could spend more time with them. Sometimes I would only get three or four hours of sleep a day. This was a big mistake for a couple of reasons. For one, it's not safe to deprive yourself of sleep. Your cognitive skills are not up to par when you don't sleep enough, and in a job like mine you want to be on your game at all times. Secondly, I noticed that I was more irritable and unhappy, so even though I was awake with the family, I wasn't much fun to be around. I eventually made some adjustments and got the proper amount of sleep that I needed. Yes, I was with my family a little less, but the quality time I did spend with them was a lot more pleasant for everyone.

The good thing is that once you begin to exercise regularly, you'll find that your sleep becomes deeper and more restorative. This is because exercise causes several beneficial changes in the body, all of which increase the quality of your sleep.[5] So even when you're not getting as much sleep as you normally do, the quality of sleep that you are getting is more advantageous to your overall health.

THE MIND

Proper sleep and exercise are essential to increasing your overall psychological health, which is just as important as your physical health.

This is a major reason that so many people meditate. The mind-body connection is something that many individuals underestimate. Although I don't practice meditation as much as I should, I do believe that meditating can have a positive effect on the body. Many people choose to meditate first thing in the morning to clear their minds and center themselves before they start their day. It makes sense, because if you're fixated on something negative that happened earlier that morning or even the night before, you're not going to be able to focus the same way a person with a clear head can.

In addition to exercise and meditation, many other activities stimulate and increase the capabilities of your mind. One of those activities is reading on a regular basis. People who read often are generally more interesting conversationalists. When you read a good book, you naturally have a desire to talk about it with others. In my experience, people who read regularly are more comfortable at social events, since they not only have an extensive vocabulary, they also have more things to talk about. Readers tend to have interesting stories and can recall information to support their statements while providing opinions and observations. By expanding their knowledge, they're more confident in their abilities to express their views, which builds trust with the listener as an authority on the topic. That confidence, coupled with the proper delivery, creates an overall better communicator.

I love the fact that if you want to learn about a particular activity, from web design to bass fishing, you can usually find it in a book. And although you may not become an expert on it after merely reading about it, you can usually become knowledgeable enough to at least hold a conversation about it. One of my best friends, Patrick, will read about something purely out of curiosity. We'll be in the middle of a conversation while drinking a beer, and he'll go off on a tangent about where the beer originated and how they came up with the name. This is clearly not the most useful information, but it's still interesting nonetheless.

Although sometimes underestimated, good conversation can stimulate the mind as well. If you're not reading books, find someone who *is* and pick their brain. When you engage with intelligent people, or simply someone who knows something that you don't, you'll expand your knowledge. If you surround yourself with people who are smarter than you, there's really only one outcome: *you'll* become smarter. Listen to what they have to say, learn from them, and you'll expand your mental library. It doesn't take a genius to figure that one out.

This next practice you should be undertaking is pretty self-explanatory, but it's worth mentioning, since many people still don't take advantage of it. Continuing your education after starting a career is advantageous no matter what you do for a living. And yes, you read that right. I said *after* you start your career. It's a no-brainer that you should go to school before getting a full-time job, but after doing so, many people devalue the importance of furthering their education. School is one of the most effective ways to keep your mind growing and developing.

Too often, we think of school as an inconvenience and are just counting down the days until we graduate. I was one of those people. Before starting the police academy, I had my associate's degree. I had planned on transferring to Roger Williams University for my bachelor's degree, but when the police department called, I couldn't drop my textbooks fast enough.

However, once I was on the job and working, I had an unfinished feeling about my education. I felt that I had sold myself short, and although I loved my job, I soon regretted not staying in school. I also thought about my kids and what they would say: "Dad, you didn't get your bachelor's. Why should I?"

Those doubts were enough to make me re-enroll in night classes at Roger Williams, where I eventually graduated. Want to know the funny part? I actually enjoyed night school. I liked it so much that after graduating I decided to diversify and expand my knowledge in a different area of study. The next semester I enrolled at Salve Regina University, where I eventually received my master's in business management. Now, I can't wait for the day when one of my daughters complains about having to go to school. I'll be pulling my degrees from the closet and placing them on full display.

In all seriousness, I'm glad I made the decision to continue my education. I gained that feeling of accomplishment I had been lacking, expanded my knowledge, and made myself more balanced as a person. My education caught up to my communication skills, allowing me to rely more on knowledge and less on actual words.

The bottom line: both your mind *and* your body are equally important, and neither works as well without the other. A sound mind in a sound body was the core value of the ancient Greeks, and staying sharp both mentally and physically will put you in a position to succeed when taking on new challenges.[6]

MONEY *CAN* BUY HAPPINESS

If you and I were having a friendly conversation about what's important in life, I wouldn't let the conversation end until I had told you what I think about money.

I know that some people consider it materialistic to look at how much money someone has in order to evaluate their status. I respectfully disagree with that sentiment. No one is going to convince me that financial stability isn't a major factor in measuring success. Don't get me wrong, money isn't *everything*, but it sure makes life a lot easier for those who have it.

The people who claim that a desire for money is a sign of materialism are saying that money shouldn't be the sole purpose of your existence, and I agree with that. I also value intellectual accomplishments, emotional achievements, and family relationships. But in order to obtain most of the good things in life, money can be instrumental, and in some cases, it's absolutely necessary. Wealth gives you the advantage of obtaining the things you want while also eliminating the stress associated with being unable to meet your financial obligations. That freedom allows you to focus the majority of your attention on self-improvement.

Again, I want to make it clear that I'm not saying our lives should revolve around making as much money as possible or that you cannot be successful *without* large sums of money. What I am saying is that it's important to seriously think about wealth and to take appropriate steps to secure the funds needed to accomplish your personal ambitions. There are effective steps that we can all take to assist ourselves in achieving wealth in our lifetime, and we can do it without becoming overly obsessed with or controlled by dollars and cents.

THE VALUE OF MONEY

The first step may seem obvious, but in many cases people fail to recognize the value of money because they're not yet responsible for their own finances or they are not constrained by a budget. If you're a young adult still living with your parents, you may not see the value in earning money since you don't have a lot of expenses. You also have extremely creative people who fail at monetizing their talent because they're so caught up in achieving their artistic aspirations. Then you have professional athletes who don't consider the future and spend their money as soon as they get it. This is a story we see all too often with pros. A talented athlete signs a huge contract and buys everything they ever wanted. The problems arise when the checks stop coming but the bills continue. It doesn't mean that the individuals aren't smart, but when *your* name is on the checks, it's *your* responsibility to know your financial status, and that all starts with understanding the value of money.

Young people living at home can still take the time to think about their future and realize that it's a good idea to plan ahead. Use the advantage of having no bills as an opportunity to save, and put yourself in a better position when you do decide to move out. Artists can follow their artistic endeavors while being mindful of the necessity of earning a living. Use that creative brain and find ways to take what you love and make money from it. And it's okay for professional athletes who earn large sums of money to seek out financial advisors, lawyers, and accountants who can guide them in planning for their eventual retirement. See what I said there? They can *guide* them, not do it *for* them. In many cases, a retiring athlete can segue into another career, which can still provide for them financially, although it may not be at the level where they need someone to manage their money. This is the time in their career when the knowledge they gained while making the big money will be extremely beneficial. If they were able to handle their finances when they were receiving and paying out large sums of bucks, taking care of smaller bills and smaller paychecks won't be a problem.

WEALTH IN CONTEXT

Money and wealth are not fixed quantities, they're fluid and changeable, and our approach to earning, saving, and spending needs to relate to our personal context. This is why it's useful to make periodic assessments of our financial situation, so that we can take an active role in preserving our monetary resources and ensuring their continued existence. For example, a person without employment may be in a predicament where acquiring some form of income immediately is critically important to their survival. On the other hand, someone who is not currently earning money might be in a position where they're still able to buy whatever they want without concern. Both of these scenarios contain conditions that will change from time to time and from person to person. Putting wealth in context based on the individual's current circumstance will allow for a better understanding of what "wealth" means to them.

DISCIPLINED SAVING

The third step in achieving financial stability is to be disciplined in how we save. This is one of the most challenging things for Americans, while people in other countries often do a better job at putting money in the bank. The sad truth is that we live in a culture that encourages the accumulation of debt and living beyond our means.[7] Most people have multiple credit cards and significant loans. Americans save only about 5 percent of their income. But if we took a lesson from the Swiss, who save more than 15 percent, we would retain a larger portion of our income and experience less financial strain.[8]

There are numerous ways to be financially disciplined, and they're all worth considering. One way is to take a fixed percent from your paycheck and put it in a separate savings account. Another idea is to set aside a specific amount for a particular goal, maybe for something you want to purchase. This way you can buy it outright rather than on credit. You can also save by reducing your spending on luxury items, which will leave you with a larger percentage of your income to put toward your bills or into an emergency fund.

I was able to put a large sum of money into a savings account when I won $575,000 on *Big Brother*. Money has become less of a burden for me these days, but I still add additional funds to that same account each month. You might be saying, "Well, of course *you* do. It's easy when you have more than half a million dollars to play with." And you would be right. It *is* a lot easier. But before going on the show, when I was living paycheck to paycheck on a sergeant's base salary, I *still* made sure I put money away each month. It may not have been as much as I do now, but it was still something. The goal here is to put enough money away to cover all of your bills for at least three months. In fact, many financial experts now say that we should aim for a cushion of eight months, and I agree with them.[9] You never know what type of emergency situation will come up and cause you to dip into your savings unexpectedly. I can't tell you how many times that extra money saved me when one of my dogs decided to swallow a toy.

I have a saying that summarizes my feelings on financial security: *money can't buy love, but it sure can buy happiness.* You may not like the sound of that, but how can you argue with that philosophy? Regardless of your current situation, money *can* buy genuine happiness with a small stroke of luck or a smart financial investment. Think about it. Say we have a guy who's poor, unhappy, and alone. The next day he finds a lottery ticket and wins a million dollars. You think he's going to be happy? Sure, his elation might only be temporary, or it might lead to something that lasts forever, but make no mistake about it: it's real. A sudden change in financial status and personal mind-set can play an integral role in building a stronger headquarters. It also creates the possibility to pursue long-term goals that weren't plausible without monetary resources.

Being financially stable can impact all aspects of your life, including improving your social interactions. Many individuals equate money with success, and people like to be around successful people. In some instances, financial security will actually take precedence over appearance or personality, making you more appealing as a romantic partner. I'm not saying I agree with that rationale, but we can't deny that we've all seen examples of it. That's the type of power money has. It can literally alter a person's perception. It has the ability to change their opinions on their own beliefs and values.

Admittedly, money isn't the only thing that makes the world go round, but it sure can make life a whole lot easier if you have it and a whole lot harder if you don't. If you have a choice, which you do, make money a result of your success, not an obstacle to achieving it.

YOU ARE THE COMPANY YOU KEEP

All three core values discussed in this chapter are essential to having a strong personal foundation, but I believe the most important one is family. When I use the term "family," I'm not just referring to blood relatives or spouses. The people you surround yourself with, which includes close friends, are usually a good indication of who *you* are as a person. These individuals also play an important role in determining what level of success you're able to reach. Successful people surround themselves with a good team. Whether they're an actor, singer, or the CEO of a large company, most of them attribute their success to the family support they receive.

If you watched *Big Brother,* you know that my main motivation for winning was my family. What most of you don't know is that there was an exact moment in the game when it went from being fun to all business. I remember sitting on the couch when we were about halfway through the game. The host, Julie Chen, came onto our screen and gave us a surprise. She informed us that she had video messages from our loved ones. When it was my turn, I got to see my wife and daughter. What really struck a chord was hearing my daughter tell me that she loved me and that she missed me for the very first time. I won't lie, I bawled my eyes out right then and there on national TV, but I honestly didn't care. After hearing those words, I knew the only way I was leaving that house was as a winner. *That's* the type of impact family support can have on a person's mentality.

In my own dealings with families while working as a police officer, I saw a trend develop where it became fashionable to dismiss or downplay the family's importance. I feel like older generations had more respect for their parents, and now I see a lot of situations where teenagers or young adults discount the need for family connections. Although that may be socially acceptable today, most of these individuals will eventually create their own families. This is when they come full circle and realize how critical their family was to their personal growth.

It's easy to take your family for granted. I've been guilty of it myself. We become busy with life and fail to make the people who formulate our foundation a priority. But when you're faced with the possibility of losing your loved ones, you get a rare opportunity to see their true value.

It was 2013, and I had recently taken a promotion from the special investigations unit as a detective to sergeant of the patrol division. One night after working the graveyard shift, I was leaving the station when the major abruptly stopped me in the hallway. He was usually pretty upbeat, but during this encounter he had this somber look on his face, and all he could say was, "The chief needs to see you in his office right now." My first reaction was, "Shit. What did I do wrong?" I was trying to get a read on the major as we walked to the chief's office, but he didn't even look at me. When we arrived, the chief was behind his desk, and the lieutenant of the detective division, Dorian Rave, was sitting in one of the chairs to his left. Lieutenant Rave was my former boss and one of my best friends. The fact that he was in the chief's office as well really surprised me. That's when I knew that this was about more than discipline.

The chief took a second to collect his thoughts and then proceeded to give me the bad news:

"Derrick, I'm going to cut right to the chase. Dorian received some intelligence from the prison that one of the inmates who you arrested is planning to kill you when he's released in a few weeks. From what we understand, his crewmembers have already obtained the guns, which are hidden in a plastic bag along the riverbed near your house. We were able to confirm that he does in fact know where you live and has described your house to his associates. I'm sorry to be the one to give you this information, but we wanted to tell you as soon as we confirmed that it was credible."

I really didn't know what to say. I was afraid and angry at the same time. To be honest, I wasn't even concerned about my own safety. The first things that came to my mind were my wife and newborn baby, both living in the house that this criminal was planning to attack when he got out. I wasn't going to let that happen.

The police department and the Rhode Island State Police were extremely helpful through the whole ordeal. A twenty-four-hour detail was placed on my house, and my family was moved to an undisclosed location for almost two weeks.

I can't get into the details about the inmate for privacy reasons, and unfortunately we were unable to charge him with a crime without exposing the confidential informant, which I didn't want to do. I can tell you that law enforcement officials spoke to the inmate about the situation, and they informed him that they knew what he had been planning. After their conversation, he decided it would be in his best interest to leave the state for a while. I crossed paths with this individual a few years later off duty, and all I can say is that we had a man-to-man conversation, and we both understood each other very clearly by the end of our discussion.

That entire ordeal was the worst two weeks of my life. I felt helpless. I wanted to handle the investigation myself, but I couldn't because of how close I was to the situation. I was beating myself up over the fact that my work had put my family in danger. My biggest concern was that I could potentially lose one of them because of *my* actions. Sitting in our temporary home with no TV and very few of our belongings reminded me of something that I had lost sight of: when it came to what really mattered to me, it wasn't about money or personal possessions; those two people were the most important things in my life.

Your family is a major component of your foundation. It's empowering to have the reassurance that no matter what happens, your family will be there for you. This is why successful people aren't afraid to fail. They know that regardless of the outcome, the people they care about, their family, will always have their back.

Formulating your own family involves developing relationships, and although it can be emotionally trying at times, there are many benefits to meeting new people and exposing yourself to different cultures. The more people you meet, the more prepared you'll be to handle unique personalities. It's an important step in finding stability and developing your confidence as an individual.

When we have good relationships with those close to us, we have a natural emotional foundation that we can draw from to deal with the stressors of life and business. This is why it's so important to reciprocate that support with family and friends. Be there for them, and they'll be there for you.

For what it's worth, here's a piece of advice that's helpful in both romantic relationships and solid friendships: *Listen*... That's all. When in doubt—just *listen* to them. Whether it's about something good or something bad, simply lend an ear.

The friendships you form throughout your life are very important for a number of reasons. To start with, these people are your "go-tos." There may not be a biological connection, but you hand-selected these individuals to be part of your team, and they should all make some type of contribution to your personal growth. If they don't, they probably shouldn't be there. Remember, the stronger the bond, the stronger your support system is, generating stability within your personal headquarters.

Above all, make sure you surround yourself with positive people. If you aspire to do great things, ensure that those around you represent the same ambitions. They should be trustworthy, dependable, and goal-oriented individuals who want success for you as much as you want it for yourself.

Good family and good friends—these are commodities that you can't put a price on. They are the difference-makers in our lives. I believe that good things happen to good people. So surround yourself with as many of them as you can and hope that it's contagious.

When we talk about health, wealth, and family, it's interesting to think that they're three completely separate entities, and yet they still have a direct effect on each other. If your home life is off, it's going to affect your performance at work, which will then affect your wallet, which can also cause stress on the mind and body. It's a domino effect. They're all connected and therefore equally essential.

Having people you can trust, physical health you can depend on, and the financial resources to take chances is the blueprint for a productive headquarters. Review where you stand with respect to each of these three fundamental areas of success, and be honest! If you make excuses, the only one you're hurting is yourself. Figure out what you can do to upgrade your current situation.

Take stock of yourself. Going through your health, wealth, and family checklist periodically can have a profound impact on your quality of life. And keep that list to yourself. Make adjustments and see if anyone notices the difference. Consider it your undercover advantage.

CHAPTER FOUR

||||||||||||||||||||||||||||||||||||||||||||||||||||||

SET YOUR SIGHTS

Setting your sights is a term we often use in law enforcement to describe lining up the sights of your firearm with a target. If you want to hit a target consistently, you need to have complete focus while aligning your front and rear sights on whatever you're aiming for. Take a breath and slowly squeeze the trigger. This is one of those rare moments when it's okay to have tunnel vision. Block everything else out. For those few seconds, nothing else matters. Don't take your sights off the target until you hit what you're aiming for.

What I'm describing is an action that often takes place at a shooting range, but it can also be interpreted as a metaphor for accomplishing your goals. Whether it's at work or in your personal life, you can set your sights on **objectives** that ultimately help you accomplish your overall **mission**. Just like the shooting range, setting your sights properly will determine how accurately and quickly you're able to accomplish these objectives, which consist of smaller tasks or assignments. By devoting all of your attention to each objective you set for yourself, you'll complete your tasks with more consistency.

Both successful and unsuccessful people are aware of the importance of hitting your marks, but the successful differ from the unsuccessful in one critical respect. Yes, both types of individuals have dreams and ambitions, but what separates them is that successful people know how to turn their personal, educational, and professional goals into accomplishments. They're not going into a situation where they're shooting blindly and merely hoping that they'll hit what they're aiming to achieve. They know what objectives they need to tackle in order to complete their overall mission.

Once you've set your objectives, how do you make them a reality? The best way I can answer that question is by showing you how we do it in law enforcement, how the most prominent leaders in business have done it, and how you can incorporate the same ideology and habits into your own life. Learning from successful people is the key to becoming successful yourself, and that's the mind-set behind how I determine who I want to emulate. I research people that I aspire to be like, learn how they go about completing their goals, and then take things from each one of them that I want to integrate into my own approach.

Through my own trial and error, I have learned that there are three main components to achieving your objectives and the overall mission. These different factors of success come into play after you've set your goals and are in a position to go after them.

The three main components are:

Knowing Your Mission

- How does completing each objective contribute to getting one step closer to your end game?

Having a Specific Ops Plan

- Before attempting to carry out a mission, it's imperative that you plan ahead. Don't simply approach a situation by firing downrange, hoping that one of the bullets hit what you're aiming for.

Focusing on One Objective at a Time

- If you're thinking about the next task before finishing the first one, your precision will be off. Take the time to make adjustments if

needed. Lock in those sights and tune everything else out. Become a sniper. Make every
shot count.

WHAT'S THE MISSION?

What are you hoping to accomplish? Is it to be accepted into your
desired university? Is it to be hired by a great company? Or is there
a person you would like to get to know better? Whatever your
intention is, before you can put a plan into action, you need to
establish a clearly defined mission so that you fully understand the
overall goal. Your mission should spell out exactly what you want
to do, and don't be afraid to state it in concrete terms. *I want to
get into Harvard. I want to work for Apple. I want to date Jessica Alba.*
Okay…the last one might take a little more than a defined mission,
but you get the point.

Almost all major corporations have a mission statement that
clearly outlines the overall goals of the company. It's no coincidence that many of these businesses are run by some of the smart-
est, most successful people in the world. If a mission statement
is good enough for them, don't you think it's good enough for
you? Having an overall mission allows you to pause for a moment
and survey things from higher ground, offering a clearer picture of
your current course and an opportunity to make adjustments.

I've always looked to people I admire to draw inspiration for my own approach. When it comes to seeing the overall vision, in my opinion nobody did it better than Steve Jobs. As one of the founding members of Apple, Jobs wanted the company to exemplify simplicity. And every design he was part of was geared toward that ultimate goal. With the release of the iPhone 7 and the decision to remove the headphone jack, it appears that Job's vision is still very much alive, even though he passed away in 2011. What made him one of the greatest minds in recent history was his ability to see a future involving a technology that hadn't been created yet. Regardless of what people around him thought, he knew what he wanted Apple to represent and how he was going to achieve it. He was on a mission.

In law enforcement, the mission is straightforward and easily understood. With statements like "We want to have a crime-free zone near the schools" or "We want to decrease theft rates in District Two," it's very clear to everyone what we intend to accomplish. And yes, the mission can still change down the line, but for the most part, these statements serve as a global description of what needs to be done. We use the concept of a mission to orient officers to the specifics they should attempt to achieve while on duty.

This concept of creating missions is a powerful tool that can be employed in both the public and private sectors as a benchmark for employees to follow. It also serves as a means to increasing productivity and monitoring progress. In the business world, a mission could involve a number of different objectives, from increasing sales to expanding publicity for a product or obtaining higher levels of customer satisfaction. On a personal level, it could include learning a new vocation, improving your physical health, or putting money aside for your child's college fund.

No matter where we are, how old we may be, or what we have going on in our lives, everyone should be on their own personal mission. It may be something inconsequential, or it may be something life-changing. Either way, the actions you are taking on a daily basis should be in line with the vision you have for yourself and your future. Some people fail to do this. They wake up and go through the motions with no real direction. If you ask yourself, "What am I doing today to improve my current situation?" and you don't have an answer, you're doing something wrong.

HAVE AN OPS PLAN

We're all creatures of habit. Some of us are more set in our ways than others, but we all have certain patterns of behavior that make us who we are. The value of being aware of this human characteristic is that we can create a game plan that places us in a more successful pattern of conduct. I really do believe that we're all presented with opportunities throughout our lives that allow us to plan ahead for what's coming. And I'm not saying that just to put an optimistic spin on life or because it sounds good.

Developing a game plan has been repeatedly proven in many different settings to be the best approach to controlling your own fate. Being adequately prepared for a situation as opposed to winging it gives you the advantage of knowing what to expect and the best way to handle it. When you prepare in advance for a job interview, it demonstrates a level of enthusiasm for the position while also giving the impression that you know what you're talking about. If you chose not to educate yourself prior to the interview, don't expect a call back.

Honestly, I feel sorry for the people who fail to prepare. It's pure laziness and a clear example of not taking a vested interest in your future. Yes, there are occasions where you have to adjust on the fly. If anyone knows that, it's a cop. But if you know your ultimate goal, why wouldn't you take the time to plan a route that is not only the most beneficial, but also the most efficient? People say that sometimes you have to experience failure before you reach success. Well, what if you could limit those failures by thinking ahead? Don't leave it to chance. Set your sights on what you want and then develop a game plan to get it.

To help us set our sights on a specific mission, we in the police community use an **ops plan**, which is short for operational plan.

Ops plans are developed before executing search warrants, making an undercover drug purchase, carrying out a prostitution sting, or for any other situation that involves multiple moving parts. The purpose of an ops plan is to turn your vision into a tangible reality that you can look at, review, and adjust if needed. It not only gives you a visual of what the end game is, it turns the overall mission into a series of strategic actions that, if carried out correctly, will result in a positive outcome. It's basically a road map to success. Who wouldn't want that?

When I created an ops plan, it consisted of a few different parts. First, I would describe the overall mission. For the purpose of this example, let's say we're executing a narcotics search warrant at 13 Watson Street. The target is John Doe, and he's selling large amounts of cocaine. The mission is to apprehend the bad guy and find the drugs. To accomplish that mission, we have a series of objectives, which consist of gaining entry into the building without being detected, locating and detaining all individuals inside the house, and searching the entire property until we find the drugs, paraphernalia, and possibly weapons. So, what's the best way to do this?

I'd start by listing all the members involved in the operation and what their specific responsibilities are. This way, they not only know what they're doing, but everyone else involved knows as well. They'd be provided with a photo of the suspect and anyone else who might be in the house. I'd also indicate where the drugs may be located, whether the suspect is armed, the presence of any dogs, and whether children may be in the home. I'd include every possible piece of information that I have, so that we're all on the same page. This level of specificity and detail gives us a huge advantage. We know exactly what we're walking into before even stepping foot into the house; meanwhile, the suspect is still in bed, dreaming about what he's going to do with all of his money.

Writing down what you intend to do in an ops plan can lead to better execution, but that doesn't only apply to law enforcement. The same approach can be utilized in almost any situation that involves an overall mission with multiple steps. Whether it's a personal or professional goal, creating your own ops plan will be time well spent. And it doesn't matter how far in advance you need to plan for something, utilizing an ops plan to develop a strategy works well for both short-term and long-term goals.

Here's an example of a business ops plan for a short-term goal. Imagine you own a business and you're planning to host a one-day charity event. You're expecting twenty-five to fifty people to attend. By planning ahead, you can determine how many employees you need, how large of a location is required, and how much food to order. Visually, it would look something like this:

"SAVE A CHILD" CHARITY EVENT

Objective: Raise $5,000 to donate to the Rhode Island

Children's Hospital

Location: Higginson Park

Time: 5:00 p.m.–9:00 p.m.

Expected Attendance: 25–50 people

Assignments:

> Samantha–Host

> Kim–Greeting and directing attendees

> John–Serving food

> James and Lisa–Auctioneers

As you can see, developing an ops plan for a short-term mission doesn't take a lot of time. The hour it takes to draw up a plan like this will probably save you a day of aggravation. By putting it on paper, everyone knows that the goal is to raise a minimum of five thousand dollars to donate to the Rhode Island Children's Hospital, and two of the objectives that need to be completed to make that happen are serving food and hosting an auction. You've now created a clear and concise description of the overall mission and what's expected from the rest of your team.

Developing an ops plan for a short-term mission is a great way to stay on course, but it's even more of an asset when developing a plan for a long-term mission. When you set a goal for yourself that may take months, maybe even years to accomplish, it's easy to get off track. Having something to refer back to and measure your progress is crucial.

There's a quote from Leonardo da Vinci that expresses my feelings on planning for the future. Da Vinci said, "People of accomplishment rarely sat back and let things happen to them. They went out and happened to things."[10] Nobody owes you anything. If you want it, make it happen for yourself. And that starts by developing a blueprint to make that far-off dream a reality.

Here's another example of an ops plan; this one is for a long-term goal. In this scenario, you're a sophomore in high school, and you know that you have a few years of school left, but you're determined to become a veterinarian. You've done your research and know that one of the top veterinary schools in the country is the Cummings School of Veterinary Medicine at Tufts University. It's not easy to get into a program like that, so you need to figure out what you can do *now* to put yourself in a better position than your competition. My motto is, "While everyone else is sleeping, you're working." And this is one of those circumstances where going the extra mile may turn out to be the difference-maker for you. So, what would an ops plan for a high school student looking to get into a prestigious university look like? If it were me, it would look something like this:

VETERINARY SCHOOL

School: **Tufts University**

Enrollment Year: **2016**

Acceptance Rate: **14%**

Average SAT Score: **1340**

Tuition: **$51,304 per year**

Objectives

Educational:

> Maintain a GPA of 3.7 or higher

> Earn a minimum of 1400 on SATs

> Take all college preparatory classes

Financial:

> Save funds from part-time job

> Learn about possible scholarships

> Apply for financial aid

Extracurricular:

> Volunteer at local zoo or animal shelter

> Apply for internship at local veterinary clinic

So there it is. A visual breakdown of the objectives you need to complete in order to increase your odds of being accepted at the school of your choice.

Note that I researched some information about Tufts University to find out what I was up against. Preparation is integral for any ops plan: reviewing the layout of a drug house; investigating the background of a gang member; or (in this case) researching the requirements for a university. The scenarios are different, but the ops plan template remains the same.

And although some ops plans may take years to materialize, *that's* what makes it so special. To see a long-term plan come to fruition after years of research and hard work will give you a feeling of satisfaction that you have to experience for yourself to really appreciate. Don't be the person who's sitting there saying, "I wish I had known about that sooner." Look ahead, anticipate what's next, and control your own destiny.

WHAT'S PLAN B?

I'm a realist. I understand that no matter how much you prepare, sometimes things don't go according to plan. Unforeseen circumstances are even more common with long-term goals because we're trying to anticipate scenarios far in advance. When developing your personal ops plan, as the great Julie Chen would say, "Expect the unexpected." The best way to counteract those unexpected circumstances is to have a contingency plan.

Whenever I developed an ops plan for a criminal investigation,

I always attached a contingency plan that listed the possible problems that could occur and how to deal with them. While I didn't anticipate any negative things happening, if they did, we were ready for them.

Hope for the best, but prepare for the worst. Best-case scenario, you don't need a backup plan. Worst-case scenario, you do, *but* now you know how to handle whatever it is you're facing. To give you a better understanding of what I'm talking about, here's the actual contingency plan that I used while working as a detective in the special investigations unit.

Shots Fired Prior to Entry

- React to threat
- Establish perimeter or move to rally point
- If necessary, withdraw and set up exterior perimeter
- Account for all personnel
- Team leader to establish command post with additional responding unit

Officer Down—Interior or Exterior

- React to threat
- Establish cover; provide additional cover during rescue
- Maintain position if possible or withdraw and establish perimeter

- If necessary, move to rally point
- Account for all personnel
- Team leader to establish command post with additional responding unit

Hostage Situation

- React to threat
- Establish perimeter
- If immediate danger, initiate rescue
- If shots are fired, announce whoever or whatever has been shot

Tactical Concerns

- Work in pairs
- React to threat
- Announce cleared rooms
- Do not enter or exit via rear doors
- Do not move beyond assigned area

Now, as you can probably imagine, everyone involved with the operation hated reading this page because it addressed some of their biggest fears. And that's okay. I'd rather them have these possible scenarios in the back of their minds, so that if the worst does arise, everyone knows what to do.

Let's look at the example I gave previously about planning a charity event. The ops plan is based on an estimated attendance of twenty-five to fifty people. But what if a hundred people show up? Although you may not expect it, you still have to prepare for it. In this case, the contingency plan would be to reserve a location that can handle that many people, have three additional employees on standby, and have the food vendors bring extra meals in case the crowd is larger than expected. Although this is a good problem to have, especially when you're raising money for charity, you don't want the lack of preparation to be more of a focal point than the cause itself.

Even with perfect planning, there may be some bumps in the road. Truth is, no matter what you do or how much you prepare, sometimes things occur that you didn't anticipate. The people who embrace this fact of life don't fear adversity. They know that if they're thrown a curveball, they can still hit it out of the park.

ONE AT A TIME

When we're in the zone and ready to go after the things we want in life, it's easy to take on too much at once. We know where we want to be and that there are some things we need to do before getting there. So instead of taking them on one at a time, we try to juggle multiple tasks. Can you get away with it? Absolutely. People do it every day. Hell, I do it all the time. Just like a lot of people out there, I'm impatient. I don't want to wait until tomorrow to tackle the next task. I'm ready to go right now.

Does that sound like you? If it does, that's good. Keep that hunger. That's something you can't teach. What it comes down to is finding a balance between ambition and ability. You don't want to become overzealous and take on more than you can handle. Not only will that decrease your quality of work, it'll increase your chances of failure.

At the time of writing this, I was driving with my wife, Jana, and my daughters, Tenley and Peyton, to the doctor's office. The weather was changing here in Rhode Island, and it was that time of year when everyone gets sick. Both my daughters had colds, so we wanted the doctor to check them out to make sure everything else was okay. While we drove, I mentioned to Jana that we really needed more closet space. I had found a really nice setup at IKEA that would essentially give us a second closet in our bedroom. I was talking about the layout and how I could demo the wall, add the new closet, and then reframe and add Sheetrock around it. I like doing that kind of stuff, and I was really getting excited talking about it. Then my wife said something that made me stop and reconsider. "With everything going on right now, do you seriously think you have time for that?"

I was still flying back and forth from Rhode Island to Los Angeles to finish filming, I was working midnights at the police station, and I was writing this book. On top of all that, I was also handling all the details for our trip to Disney World in fifteen days. After taking a second to think about it, my response was simple: "No, probably not."

Now, in all probability, could I have built the closet? Sure. But at what cost? If you add to the list of tasks you've already set for yourself, you're limiting the amount of time you have for each one. The result is an outcome that is not reflective of your capability. So how would it have affected me? I could've seen a reduction in my productivity at work. My writing could have suffered. Or maybe the door on my new closet would have fallen off six weeks after I installed it. You can avoid these negative outcomes if you remind yourself to take on one objective at a time. Do yourself a favor and eat what's already on your plate before going for seconds.

We've talked about short-term and long-term ops plans, but what about daily agendas? What we do day to day dictates whether or not we'll reach our weekly, monthly, and even yearly goals. If you focus your firepower on one assignment at a time, you'll have a stronger impact in a shorter time span. Even though daily tasks are considered smaller steps, perhaps even unimportant ones, it's essential that they be completed with maximum effort. Getting to school on time, paying attention in class, doing all of your homework—all small steps, but when you add them up, they're major contributors to your overall performance. And how well you do in school will decide what colleges or careers you have available to you in the future. So although they may seem minor at the time, they can collectively have a major impact on your opportunities.

Sometimes even the most efficient people will find themselves stuck on an objective, because despite their best efforts, they're having trouble focusing on the task at hand. I've found that this is often the result of improper sequencing. When you're at the shooting range, aiming at one target that's fifteen feet away but already thinking about the next target that's a hundred feet away, you're more likely to miss. Before you can apply to be a lawyer, you need a law degree. If you're more focused on what law firm you want to work for than on law school itself, you may find yourself applying for an entirely different job. Compartmentalizing each objective will allow you to treat it as a separate entity, and by taking on each task sequentially, you're more likely to complete them.

I love motivational quotes. I use them as inspiration. We've all heard the saying often attributed to Hunter S. Thompson: "Anything worth doing is worth doing right,"[11] and I couldn't agree more. If you're going to do something, don't half-ass it. I'm a firm believer that everything we do, whether it's cutting the grass or writing a book, is a reflection on who we are. You never know what someone's going to judge you on, so when you take on an assignment, give it everything you have. Make it the best representation of what *you* have to offer.

Take some time to figure out what it is you want out of life, and then design an ops plan to get you there. Break down your game plan into smaller objectives so that there are minor victories along the way. Set your sights on your personal mission and trust the process. When you have a clearly defined goal, it's easy to cut out the bullshit and concentrate on what's important. Make your mission your mantra.

CHAPTER FIVE

||||||||||||||||||||||||||||||||||||||||||||||||||||||||||||||

EXERCISE YOUR RIGHT TO REMAIN SILENT...BUT LISTEN

When it comes to the ability to engage in dialogue, most people automatically assume they know what they're doing since they've been talking for most of their lives. But the ability to speak is only half the battle. In reality, the ear is the most important tool of an effective communicator.

What really separates good conversationalists from everyone else is their ability to *listen*. Paying attention to what people have to say allows you to absorb the information being relayed and respond with content in-line with whatever's being discussed. Learning to listen like a professional is crucial to cultivating the skill of reading people and developing stronger interpersonal communication methods. Even more, interpersonal skills can help you identify good situations and navigate out of bad ones. I know this from personal experience, since dealing with uncertain situations is something a police officer does on a daily basis.

I know what you're going to say: "Why would I take advice about listening from a cop, when most of the time, they're *telling* people what to do?"

I completely understand where you're coming from, and it's a fair question. As officers, we do find ourselves in situations where we have to direct people in order to get something accomplished. However, what most people don't realize is that we also receive extensive training in **verbal judo** and mediating difficult situations. It's funny, but I've always said that cops are usually at their best when the situation is at its worst. That's just the way we work. So when people are at each other's throats with no resolution in sight, we find a compromise that everyone can live with. But how do we do this if we're always *telling* people what to do? Before giving any advice, we have to understand what the problem is. This involves listening to each person and figuring out the underlying issues. From this standpoint, we can deliver our recommendations in a way that people are open to hearing.

It's unfortunate that many people view police officers as being unapproachable. This misconception is partially due to our need to project a position of authority. The ability to show strength is so vital to our job that it's ingrained in us as soon as we start the police academy. One of the first levels of force we're taught as officers is our command presence. This basically means to show everyone that we mean business, and it's done through the way we dress, our posture, and the tone of our voice. Admittedly, it's sometimes tough to turn this mentality off between calls, and this is where the whole "that cop treated me like an ass for no reason" usually comes from. I can tell you from experience that it's not personal. It's difficult to hop in and out of character for some cops. For all you know, that officer was just involved in a fight with an armed suspect and now he's dealing with your minor motor vehicle accident. Regardless of who you are, we've all been guilty of carrying over a certain demeanor to our next conversation with someone who has nothing to do with your current mood.

Although cops are human and make mistakes, I like to think that most of the time we get it right. With constant training in interpersonal communication, our ability to listen and pick up on pertinent information only increases with experience. Over the years I've learned a few key factors that are important in almost any conversation.

Do

- Do remind yourself to listen carefully.

- Do take a second before responding to gain additional information.
- Do interpret what someone is really trying to say based on *how* they say it.

Don't

- Don't think about what you're going to say next while someone else is speaking.
- Don't cut someone off in the middle of a sentence.
- Don't think of listening as an obligation. It's an opportunity to gather intelligence.

These are some of the rules I always keep in the back of my mind during a dialogue. They might seem like minor changes and easy to implement, but adjustments like these can take you from being a good listener to a great one.

RECEIVE BEFORE YOU RESPOND

Are you the type of person who meets someone new, exchanges introductions, and then an hour later you can't remember their name? If you are, this section specifically applies to you. And don't feel bad, because it used to apply to me as well. To be honest, I was one of the biggest offenders. It's so awkward to have to ask someone for their name again after hitting it off and deciding to make future plans.

The reason we get tripped up by this mistake is because we're so concentrated on what *we* are saying and doing that we completely skate over important details about the other person. We're so busy thinking about what *we* want to say next that we miss half the conversation. Do you know someone like this? You know you do. Unfortunately, we all do.

I was recently at a party with a friend and many new people were introduced to us. My friend was thoroughly enjoying himself and had been talking to a girl who he was clearly interested in. They eventually exchanged numbers, and things were going well, but then it took a turn for the worse. I almost spilled my drink from laughing when I heard him ask, "How do you spell your name so I can save it in my phone?" She looked at him with disappointment, paused for a second, and then responded with, "J—E—N." Suddenly, Jen had somewhere to be and rejoined her friends.

Don't get me wrong, my friend's a bright guy, but he definitely dropped the ball on this one, and it cost him a date.

"Hey, Nick," I said to him a few days later. "You ever hear from Jen?"

"Nah," he replied.

I laughed and grabbed him by the shoulder. "You can't forget their name in the first conversation, my man. That's not the way you want to start a relationship."

His face turned bright red. He knew he had slipped up at the party. Reluctantly he responded, "Okay, Derrick, let's hear it. Just kick me while I'm down."

I smiled and told him to relax. "Nobody is holding it against you," I said. "It's hard to remember everyone's name unless you know a few tricks."

I'm going to tell you the same thing I told him, and it all boils down to this: the key to any memory, whether it's names, dates, or just a list of things you need to remember, is making the proper associations. Memory experts, like the ones you see on television who can remember the sequence of all the cards in a shuffled deck, are able to do this by using associations to fix the cards in their memory. They're essentially using a similar version of the method I taught Nick for remembering the people he meets.

The key to remembering someone is to associate the name with a face. Probably the easiest and most effective way to do this is to look carefully at the person when you're being introduced. In those first few minutes that you're standing there talking with them, make a mental note of any features that strike you as prominent, such as the shape of their nose, their eyeglasses, any moles you might notice, or any scars or tattoos. The next thing you want to do is repeat their name two or three times while talking with them. Try to thread it right into the conversation. If they have an unusual name, make a point of asking them how they got it. Did their parents have a particular reason for choosing it? Where does it originate? While they're telling you their story, you're reinforcing your association of this person with that name.

In addition, as you observe their features, which are immutable characteristics of a person, you should quickly search in your memory for anyone you know who has some of the same physical features. It could be their hairstyle, eyes, facial structure, mouth—whatever you observe. If you can see some commonalities between the person you just met and, let's say, your friend Mary, you simply superimpose the two images and their names, making a mental association. You may even say to her, "You look like my friend Mary," to reinforce the connection. That way, when you see her again you'll automatically think of your friend Mary, and immediately remember her name.

It goes without saying that this technique requires some mental effort, and it does take a little time to learn. When you get more experience with it, you'll do it faster, just like those memory experts on television. This is because you're using information that is already stored indelibly in your long-term memory and merely tagging this new person to an existing image.

The brain can only process a small fraction of the light, sound, tactile, and other sensory impulses impinging on our input system.

The larger part of this incoming data is filtered out. However, you can train yourself to be more open to receiving new information. Concentrate on hearing and seeing what the other person is saying and doing and less on your own words and actions.

Even though we're focused on listening and observing, it's okay to interject reference questions to help clarify what the individual is saying. You do this without intentionally interrupting their flow of thought. Instead, when they pause, you say something that echoes what they've said, asking them for clarification or amplification.

When I dealt with an altercation between two colleagues at work, I would pull them aside and speak to them separately. If you're a manager, you know that simply asking the question, "What happened?" only goes so far. Employees won't usually divulge too much information out of fear of being viewed as a "whistle-blower" by their counterparts. They may say something like, "We were on a call involving a domestic disturbance between a husband and wife, and I didn't like the way it was handled by the other officer."

That's not really telling me much, so I'll interject a question along the lines of, "So what was the behavior of the two spouses like when you arrived?" I'm obviously trying to elicit the same information as before, but this signals to the officer that I'm listening and interested in hearing more about the situation. It reassures him that this is not just a formality, and that I'm genuinely interested in his point of view.

He may go on to explain that although there were no visible injuries to the wife, he still would have arrested the husband. If he knows I am really listening, he might elaborate by revealing that when he was a child, he experienced domestic violence between his parents, and the abuse only escalated after the cops left without arresting his father. With that new information, not only do I get a deeper understanding of what occurred, but my questioning has exposed an aspect of my subordinate's life that I was unaware of.

Even if the person doesn't tell you anything new, they're almost always going to repeat what they just said, giving you a chance to hear it twice while fixing it firmly in your memory. By asking someone to reaffirm or repeat their statement by rephrasing the original question, it enables you to make a more thorough assessment of their mental and emotional state in relation to the topic at hand. But don't overuse this tactic. Asking people too often to repeat themselves could leave them feeling like you weren't listening in the first place. This technique is not a necessity for every conversation, but if you're having difficulties deciphering what someone is saying, this might be a good option for you.

These are the basic principles that will get you started on the road to becoming a more attentive listener. If you make a conscious effort to associate faces with names, you'll remember the people you interact with easier. If you remind yourself to look and listen with an open mind, you'll perceive more of what someone is conveying. And if you reflect questions back to the person you're speaking with, you'll prompt them to repeat the important facts.

Keep your mind clear, concentrate on what's being said, think about what you've just heard, and *then* respond. These minor adjustments will cause you to retain more information, allowing you to get a lot more out of the conversation.

THAT AWKWARD PAUSE...

The next method we're going to talk about might sound a little unconventional at first, but if you time it right, it can be extremely useful. I started using this as a patrolman, and I found it so effective that I continued to use it as a detective during my interviews and interrogations.

It's interesting because, through all the different training and seminars I've attended, I have never heard anyone talk about using silence as a means of getting someone to talk. When I first tell people about it, they automatically think of a movie where the cop asks the suspect about a crime and they quickly respond with "I don't know anything!" The detective then sits there for a few seconds and stares at the suspect. The suspect get nervous, begins to squirm a little, and then blurts out, "All right, I did it!" Let me tell you right now: this technique is good...but it's not *that* good. I wish it were. It would have made my job a lot easier.

However, using silence as a tool will give you the upper hand in any encounter where your goal is to extract information that's being withheld. This is applicable when dealing with employees, family members, or acquaintances, or even negotiating a deal with a complete stranger. Most people genuinely enjoy social interaction and substantive conversation, feeling obliged to contribute meaningful dialogue. This helps explain why a purposeful pause is so effective in getting people to elaborate further.

When I was a patrolman, I would arrive at a call and get oriented to the situation by speaking with every person there. This usually involved some small talk, basic information about who they were, and how they became involved with the incident. Once I felt I had broken the ice, I would start asking pointed questions about the actual incident, focusing on what each person had seen and heard before, during, and after the crime had occurred. Now, keep in mind that in the city where I work, many people don't want to speak with the police out of fear of being labeled a snitch. So if you ask them what happened, they will usually try and give you just enough so that you go away. You can always peg these people pretty quickly, because as they're answering you, they're looking around to see who's watching them or they're walking away before they even finish answering the question. It always amazes me how many people are standing around when the police arrive, but as soon as they start asking questions, everyone has somewhere to be. Funny how that works...

When I encounter a witness that is willing to speak with me, I usually start with a very broad question like, "What happened?" I refer to this initial question as my umbrella question because it basically covers everything. Most of the time, people respond with something generic like, "I saw a red car take a right on Fletcher Street. Then I heard two loud bangs, and the car sped off, but that's all I know." My natural instinct is to follow up with another question, but I don't. I just wait, maintaining eye contact the whole time. The silence will almost become awkward, but sometimes the person I'm speaking with will volunteer a little more information. "There might have been two guys in the car. One was wearing a white hat. I think the first three digits of their plate were 327, but like I said, that's all I know."

As a detective, I used the same tactic during my interrogations. When I had a suspect who was holding back information, giving me only enough to suppress my appetite for the truth, I would wait for an opportunity where I really felt like they had more to say. When they stopped talking and looked at me for acknowledgment, I would quietly sit there, giving them a look that said, "Go ahead. Continue."

Essentially, what your momentary pause has done is create a level of psychological pressure that forces them to say something else in an attempt to garner a response from you. It doesn't surprise me that when there's a silence during an interview, the interviewee feels a need to fill that awkwardness with their voice. It's the natural back and forth that creates dialogue, and we learn this pattern of speaking at a very young age. It's the way we've been programmed. One person talks, and when they're done speaking, the other person responds—or at least they're expected to. So when they *don't*, the natural reaction is for the person who was originally speaking to elaborate further on what they were saying.

This psychological pressure, which is felt internally by all people during a conversation, is a very powerful tool for a detective. It has allowed me to elicit information that witnesses otherwise wouldn't reveal, and in some situations it proved to be the difference in the case. The irony is that I was able to get the answer I needed with silence, rather than with an actual question. All it takes is the conscious effort to briefly stop the flow of words out of *your* mouth, so that the other person feels an unconscious need to have them coming out of *theirs*.

To put it another way, we're playing mind games, and in some scenarios, that's perfectly okay. I think you'll be pleased with the results that this minor adjustment can produce when you're interviewing someone for a job, interacting with employees or colleagues, or even having a casual conversation with a family member or friend.

Giving the silent treatment isn't only advantageous in a work setting or during a social encounter. I used the same tactic on *Big Brother*. I would ask contestants about their feelings toward other people in the house to get a read on them. In an effort to satisfy my curiosity without divulging too much information, they would give me a quick response. Instead of immediately answering them, I would wait. There were a few occasions where they got the hint that their answer wasn't sufficient based on my reaction (or lack thereof), and it prompted them to reveal a few more details. If you watched the show, then you already know that the last piece of information they gave me was usually the most useful, and that was what I eventually used against them. Hey, give me a break! It was a game, and it was for half a million dollars. I think most people would have done the same.

My training has helped me in many ways beyond catching bad guys and winning TV shows. I recently took on a new role as an investigator on Investigation Discovery's *Is OJ Innocent? The Missing Evidence*. Some of my interviews were designed to not only help me learn more about the different aspects of the case, but to also learn more about who the victims were as people. In most police interrogations, we remove all emotional attachment and concentrate on the facts. When you're on television, it's important to create a connection between the victim and the audience. By asking questions that create a deeper understanding of each character, the viewer becomes more invested in the outcome of the show. On *The Missing Evidence*, this questioning involved speaking with family and friends, and it wasn't as easy as I thought it would be. It forced me to develop a completely new approach to getting what I needed from the interviewee. I would ask a question like, "Do you miss them?" They would quickly respond, "Of course. It's so hard with them being gone." Again, my natural instinct would be to respond with something obvious, like "I'm sorry for your loss" or "I can only imagine." But I quickly discovered that my response put an end to their answer. It gives them the false impression that you're satisfied with what they had to say. Of course they missed them, but I wanted to know more about what it was like to no longer have this person in their life.

So instead, I held off and refrained from saying anything. I gave them a few seconds to process the question. They usually looked off in the distance for a moment, breaking eye contact with me, and then continued to speak about the person. Sometimes they told a story about the victim that they just remembered, which produced new material that the viewers and I wouldn't have heard if I hadn't given them a moment to think. Not only did this technique allow me to learn more about the victim, it also resulted in some of the more memorable scenes. Those personal stories are what allowed us to see that the victim was not just a piece of evidence; they were a person with dreams and aspirations, making them relatable to everyone watching. All of that was accomplished with the use of a momentary pause.

Sure, the technique isn't 100 percent effective. It may flat-out fail in some instances. You'll find yourself staring at someone's face while they're not saying anything, and believe me, I *have*— but who cares? That small risk is worth the reward. Even in casual conversations with friends and family, you'll find it useful in getting them to open up about a topic they otherwise wouldn't discuss. In fact, I recommend trying this tactic out for the first time with someone you're comfortable with. You don't want your first attempt to be during a time when you really need it to work. Pause for a moment after the other person has had their say. See if it causes them to offer a few more words. Even though you're talking to someone you think you know pretty well, you may be surprised at the additional revelations that follow. I've seen positive results using this approach, and because of that success, the term *silent treatment* has taken on a whole new meaning for me. Eventually, it will for you too.

IT'S ALL ABOUT THE DELIVERY

One of the most important lessons I've learned is that it's not only about *what* people say, it's *how* they say it. Our attention now turns to a method of listening that can help you sharpen your understanding of what people really mean when they open their mouths. All we're doing is adding another layer to your listening skills, giving you the ability to measure a person's honesty more accurately based on what you hear in the person's intonation and delivery.

So you're paying attention. You're hearing every word they have to say. You could recite the entire conversation back word for word if you had to. That's great! It's important to pick up on the details of a conversation if you really want to understand the meaning of the discussion. But it doesn't stop there, because you can't always take people at their word. You have to not only hear what they're saying, but also the manner in which they say it.

People can speak a sentence in many different inflections and give it a whole new meaning each time. You could ask your friend, "What do you think of John?" They immediately reply directly with, "He's a great guy. Real winner." Most people would look at those words and say, "Well, clearly he's a fan of John." And that may be true, especially if he responds immediately and in a confident tone. But what if he draws out the words "great" and "real" and speaks the whole sentence with a tone of sarcasm? Now it just went from "He really likes John" to "He can't stand John" with just a minor change in delivery.

As with anything, practice makes perfect when it comes to analyzing the true feelings behind someone's words. Actors train themselves to change aspects of their voice, giving them the ability to convey various emotions even though they're reading from a script. But as a listener, you can also train yourself to hear these changes and to be more aware of them when they occur. An increased sensitivity to delivery and intonation can provide significant insight into the feelings, thoughts, and motivations of the people you encounter.

One of the ways that you can increase your sensitivity to these subtle changes in inflection is by actively listening for them when engaging in conversations with people that you know well. By consciously seeking the underlying details of what a person is actually feeling through their tone and changes in delivery, you'll learn to be a more sensitive listener, giving you a deeper understanding of a person's mind-set. Remind yourself to listen hard. Be proactive about trying to discern subtle shades of meaning in their voice. It's always interesting what you can pick up on when you're actively listening for it. The depth of feeling that is revealed by the human voice gives you an opportunity to discover things that most people overlook.

It's also important to remember that people will sometimes try to avoid talking about things that are difficult for them to face. So if you ask a question and the person tries to change the subject, it may be a sign that they're skirting around an issue that they'd rather not discuss. If you're tactful enough, you can usually find a way to bring the subject back up at a later time. Sophisticated conversationalists are able to read a person and know when to push the issue and when to pull back. They prod a bit, and when they meet some resistance, they back off for a while. They'll come back to the issue again when they see an opening. This is the same approach we take when interviewing victims, especially children. It's not an easy thing to relive the crime they were involved in, and we understand that. This is why we go at their pace, and although it may take a little longer, we eventually get the information we need by listening to what they're saying and the way in which they say it.

An interesting way to develop the listening skills required to perform that type of reactive communication is to observe your favorite actors, either on television, in films, or onstage. Actors are some of the most talented people in the world at relaying what they are feeling through their words. Denzel Washington, Meryl Streep, Tom Hanks, Viola Davis, Leonardo DiCaprio, Will Smith—these are just a few of my personal favorites, but the list is endless. I'm sure you have your favorites, so as we talk about delivery, think about them and how they were able to make you feel even though you knew it was just a movie. The most effective actors are honest and generous in their work, allowing themselves the vulnerability of genuine emotion and sharing it with others. They have an ability to dig deep into their soul and pull from personal experience to create a believable character the audience can connect with.

When I was working as an undercover detective, I realized early on that my success would depend on my ability to "play the part." Before going undercover, you're given a cover story (including a name, where you're from, and your background) and you build your "character" around those details. This is the same thing professional actors do. They take the information the script provides and develop their character into a complete person. So I knew that if I wanted to become better at my job, I needed to become a better actor, which included the ability to convey certain feelings through my words.

That's when I decided to take a basic acting course at the Trinity Repertory Company in Providence, Rhode Island. My acting coach, Fred Sullivan, was an experienced actor who I had seen in a few plays prior to signing up for the class. His performances were incredible, so I was really looking forward to learning from him. Overall, I gained a lot of insight from the class, and surprisingly, I really enjoyed it. The knowledge I took away from that experience helped me grow as an undercover detective by teaching me how to express an emotion with my voice. By understanding my own mannerisms, I also increased my ability to interpret the behavior of my target through *their* tone of voice and delivery. Although this story may sound trivial, I mention it because I believe my decision to take those acting classes was a pivotal moment in my law enforcement career.

Now, I'm not saying everyone needs to take an acting class in order to become a better listener. I fully understand that people in real life are usually not as dramatic as actors in a stage play. However, the vocal inflections displayed by those actors when conveying a certain emotion are similar to what you'll see with the people you encounter every day. But how do you know what verbal cues to look for? This is an easy question to answer, and the person you need to practice with will always be available when you need them. It's *you*!

The benefit of learning from yourself is that only *you* know how you really feel. So let's say you're with a significant other, and they tell you that they're going out with a friend that you don't really like. Physically, you may give the impression that you're okay with it, but make note of your tone. Why? Because although everyone's different, the verbal indicators *you* exhibit may be similar to what someone else would display if the topic being discussed made *them* uncomfortable or angry.

Utilize your own intonations and delivery to increase your listening skills by using your involuntary behavior as a baseline to gauge others. Does your voice ever drop to a lower level? If so, why? Do you ever raise your voice? Again, why? Do you ever hesitate or pause when talking about something that may be emotionally significant to you? These subtle variances are worth noting, because delivery can make or break a dialogue. Read a person's verbal cues correctly, and you'll get what you need. Read them wrong, and you're in for a short conversation.

Understanding the value of remaining silent and using my ability to interpret the verbal indicators projected by the people I interact with has served me well. This knowledge has been valuable to me not just as a cop, but also as a husband, a father, a brother, a friend, and in a social experiment like *Big Brother*. Now it's *your* turn.

In order to implement these same techniques during your own encounters, you must overcome your social instinct to keep the conversational ball bouncing. If you really want to hear the details, resist the urge to fill the silence with your words. Remember, even though they're doing most of the talking, you're in the driver's seat; they're just coming along for the ride.

CHAPTER SIX

||||||||||||||||||||||||||||||||||||||||||||||||||||||

FIND YOUR "SIXTH SENSE"

I know that you probably think of the 1999 film when you hear the phrase *sixth sense*, but in my approach to dealing with people, these words have nothing to do with seeing ghosts. I'm referring to the ability to read people by their body language and how to use that information to anticipate their next move. The good news is that everyone possesses this ability. It's just a matter of learning how to use it, and part of that process involves knowing what to look for.

Before you can progress, you have to understand how physical behavior relates to what a person is thinking. Anyone who has watched me on television knows I love to talk with my hands. Using your body to express what you're trying to convey is a common form of communication, as these physical mannerisms can indicate certain feelings or intentions. Many people are guilty of wearing their hearts on their sleeves, which allows you to learn a great deal about them just by watching how they interact with their surroundings. In addition to observing others, start taking note of your own reactions when you're angry, sad, or uncomfortable. Self-discovery is sometimes the best way to learn what's going through the hearts and minds of the people around you.

A real leader *motivates* people through common goals and good communication, and one of the surest ways to increase productive communication is to develop your sixth sense. It's also important to identify and categorize the different people in your life so you can determine which ones to work with and which ones to avoid. Some people will contribute to your success, while others will hinder it. The ability to know the difference is what will enable you to excel.

Being able to interpret a person's motive through their physical behavior is a necessity in today's society. There are so many people out there with an underlying agenda, but if you pay attention, you have the potential to see right through it. This understanding will create a confidence in your ability to read people, allowing you to trust your initial instinct and become a more confident communicator as you learn to master your own sixth sense.

EVERYONE HAS A SIXTH SENSE

One of the first challenges I faced as a patrolman was picking up on the subtle indicators that criminals would sometimes display. And one of my earliest experiences with reading people's behavior came during my first week on patrol with a veteran officer. We were driving through a tough area of Central Falls when Officer Rave, my partner, tapped me on the shoulder.

"Slow down," he said.

"Why?"

"The guy crossing the street. He's up to something."

"What do you mean?" I asked.

"Stop asking questions, and just slow down."

I stopped the car and we exited the vehicle. We began to walk along the sidewalk toward an open fence. As we got to the area where the unidentified male had just come from, we shined our flashlights on a storefront window and noticed that it had been broken. We subsequently discovered that a robbery had taken place only a few minutes earlier. We eventually tracked down and arrested the suspicious individual, and, fortunately for us, he still had the stolen items in his pockets.

But how did my partner know that a crime had just occurred?

The answer to that question involves an important concept in psychology that we use often in police work—and there may be a scientific term to describe this feeling of unease—but for me—it's as simple as, "something ain't right."

The mind can absorb a large amount of information on an unconscious level. We take in much more sensory data than we can consciously process, and some of that data can trigger a feeling of uneasiness. The best explanation that I can come up with in this case is that as we were approaching the scene, Officer Rave was able to see both the open fence and the questionable behavior of the suspect. Although it didn't register with his conscious mind at the time, his unconscious processed all of the information, and even though he didn't know exactly what it was, he knew something was wrong. The open fence, the suspect's avoidance of eye contact, the current lighting conditions in the area—all those visual indicators were processed by Officer Rave's brain without his being aware of it. His feelings of uneasiness, coupled with his visual observations, are what he later referred to as his *sixth sense*.

After that day, I spent a considerable amount of time developing my own sixth sense. I made a conscious effort to absorb as much information as I could about my surroundings. I would take mental notes about certain factors like the time of day, the area of the city, and the weather, and I would use that information to evaluate the behavior of the people I observed during my patrol.

For example, if I saw a person walking down the street in a commercial area, that wouldn't typically be a big deal to me. But if it's three in the morning, eighty degrees outside, and they're wearing a winter jacket and a backpack, it would definitely get my attention. Add the fact that they refused to make eye contact and then turned into a dark alley as I passed them, and you can guarantee that we'll be having a conversation.

During my time in the patrol division, I had many encounters with a variety of different people. Those experiences produced a strong foundation for me to build on, and over time my sixth sense became one of my strongest attributes. This eventually helped me progress in my career, resulting in a promotion to the Investigative Division, where I continued to work on my ability to interpret behavior.

I remember one of my earliest interrogations as a new detective, which involved an accusation of child molestation. The father was being accused of molesting his three-year-old daughter. He was well-dressed, calm, and articulate. I proceeded to watch him from a camera for a moment as he sat in the interrogation room. He didn't look nervous at all. No rubbing of his hands, no heavy breathing, no tapping of his feet—nothing. This man was cool, collected, and appeared to not have a care in the world. But even though he appeared to be calm, he had momentary glitches in his demeanor. He was twisting in his chair, and when he realized what he was doing, he would stop. He had put a piece of gum in his mouth, chewed it for a couple of minutes, and then spit it in the trash after it lost its flavor because he had been chewing on it so hard. He was only in the room for maybe ten minutes, but he had already checked his watch four times. His way of dealing with anxiety was subtle, but unfortunately for him, it was still apparent.

A few moments later, a senior detective approached me while I was watching the camera.

"He didn't do it," he said.

"How do you know?" I asked.

"Look at him. He's way too comfortable."

My response: "Not for long."

Because of his evasive behavior, I continued to conduct my interrogation with the suspect for almost two hours. He had a good alibi, but as the questioning progressed, that once-calm demeanor changed dramatically. It became evident that he wasn't as relaxed as he wanted me to believe he was. After I pointed out numerous contradictions in his statements, he finally broke down and admitted to molesting his daughter.

When I exited the interrogation room, the same senior detective I had spoken with earlier congratulated me on getting the confession. I looked at him and said, "The sixth sense took over on that one." My gut told me the guy was hiding something. That's really all your sixth sense is: a feeling based on rational thought, combined with the ability to process external factors logically. In this case, something about the father told me he did it, and the behavior I observed inside that room, even before I spoke with him, confirmed it.

If I'm being honest, some people have more of a natural ability when it comes to their sixth sense. Still, everyone—including you—can further develop this skill so that you can read the people in *your* life. I'll offer some suggestions on how to sharpen this innate ability so that you're able to develop a profile on someone using the knowledge you've learned about them. The overall goal is to help you harness your abilities so that you can use your own sixth sense to achieve more in your personal life as well as your career.

HUMAN LIE DETECTOR

No matter where you stand in the corporate hierarchy—whether you're the chief executive officer, a middle manager, or an entry-level employee—it always pays to know the people you work with. Executives can't make their organization successful unless they know how to motivate their people. Middle managers won't rise up the ranks unless they can "see" into the minds of those above and below them. New hires will never make the grade unless they learn to perceive what attributes their supervisors possess.

The same principles of observation that can improve your professional status also apply to your personal life. Whether you're starting a new relationship or looking to improve on an old one, understanding behavior and learning how people operate is a prerequisite. Knowing which friend you can trust, or which family member really has your back, comes down to being able to read their verbal and physical cues. This also holds true for normal everyday interactions, such as negotiating a price with a car salesperson or interacting with a new neighbor.

All of these scenarios revolve around understanding who you're dealing with and what their true intentions are. Does what they're saying line up with how they're acting? Do they look you in the eye when they have something to say? This is the type of human sensitivity that I referred to earlier as your *sixth sense*. And although we use this phrase in law enforcement, it's applicable in almost any environment.

In business, one of the key components of your sixth sense is being able to determine when someone is telling the truth—or lying. When you're dealing with large amounts of money, you want to know that the person sitting across from you is on the up and up.

In your personal life, you want to know that when your daughter tells you she's out with her friend Kate, she's not actually out with her "friend" Kevin. For all the dads out there, I'm sure this one is high on your list of priorities, and as a father of two girls, I can relate.

What would you say if I told you that you have a human lie detector built right into your brain? I'm "crazy," right? This is some gimmick that belongs on one of those infomercials at four in the morning. But hear me out, and let me explain how to use your own built-in lie detector to decipher truth from deception. This is not some crazy new discovery. These are the same skills and techniques that I learned during my years as an investigator and while attending numerous interview and interrogation schools. All we're doing is translating those same skills over to the private sector and your personal life.

For a detective, it's imperative to know whether a suspect is being honest. The sad fact is that most suspects who are brought in for an interview make the conscious decision to lie. If the suspect was involved in a stabbing, they'll probably lie and say they didn't do it. They might even go so far as to deny even knowing the victim at all. And in some cases, there's no real physical evidence to prove otherwise, and they know it. They'll create an elaborate story to explain where they were and how they couldn't have possibly been involved. They may even shed a few tears. Trust me, I've seen it. So with people willing to go to this extent to deceive, how does a detective figure out the truth?

Law enforcement has evolved over the years, and investigators have developed techniques for handling people who are trying to pull one over on us. There are specific methods that we now use to find out whether a person is being truthful or deceitful. No, this is not like what you see on television, where the cop figures out the truth just by looking at the suspect, although sometimes I wish it were that easy. The methods *we* use are not foolproof, but they're highly sophisticated, and they allow us to make accurate predictions about a suspect's guilt or innocence.

So how do you know if they're lying? To figure it out, there are a couple of things that need to happen during a conversation with someone you think is misleading you. First, you observe them carefully without tipping them off that you're looking for specific actions to develop a baseline for their normal behavior. Then, you make inferences about their truthfulness based on what you observe when they talk about general topics or answer non-intrusive questions. As you're developing your final conclusions, your questioning should remain subtle. Don't make it obvious that your inquiries have an underlying purpose. Keep them off balance by switching up your delivery throughout the conversation.

In my line of work, the approach we take is a little more aggressive, and in most cases it's no secret what we're trying to accomplish. The first thing we do as investigators is bring the suspect into the interrogation room. This allows us to question them in a controlled environment. I'm sure you've seen this on TV or in the movies: the detective begins by talking to the suspect in a friendly manner, without asking any pointed or threatening questions. Our goal at this initial stage is not just to have the suspect relax, but to have them feel confident enough to speak openly. This is why we begin by talking about the suspect's personal information (name, date of birth, address), and then transition to topics like the weather or a sporting event that recently occurred. Basically anything that would entice them to answer honestly. These nonthreatening questions are commonly referred to as **control questions**. These are the questions that we know the suspect won't lie about. They'll usually engage in conversation at this point due to their false impression that there's no significant correlation between the current conversation and the crime they were brought in for. In fact, we'll make a conscious effort not to mention the crime at all during the initial dialogue.

While we're talking with the suspect, we are carefully observing their body language: the way they sit, the way they move their hands, what they do with their eyes and mouth, their breathing, and any other mannerisms they make during the questioning. When we ask a nonthreatening question like "What do you think about the Red Sox?" the suspect has no reason to lie and knows there are no consequences as a result of their answer. Yes or no, they like the team or they don't. No matter what they say, they're probably telling the truth. So we observe what their body language tells us while they're giving an honest answer. We do this so that when we ask more direct questions about the crime itself, we can note any discrepancies in how they react when their answers *do* have consequences.

So how do we know a suspect is lying when they claim they've never met the victim? Well, we don't, but—and this is a big but—we do sometimes get an indication based on the physical cues they display when asked about the victim. If they nervously tap their feet, rub their hands together, or stare at the ground every time we mention the victim's name, we make a mental note. We call each of these quirks a **tell**, a term commonly used in poker. My definition of a tell is an involuntary movement or action on the part of the individual that is out of character and not observed during control questions. This uncharacteristic mannerism *tells* me that the suspect is lying, or, at a minimum, anxious about the topic that's being discussed.

It is important to keep in mind that the appearance of some mannerisms may be coincidental. The suspect might have something in their eye, causing them to blink a lot. They may have a dry throat, resulting in an extensive amount of coughing. But once they fix the issue—remove the particle from their eye, take a drink of water—they may not exhibit that behavior for the remainder of the conversation. In that case, it's not really a tell, it's just a reaction to an outside influence. This is why detectives will vary their questioning throughout the interview, moving from control questions to specific questions about the crime. When the officer observes a tell, they'll note it and return back to casual conversation and nonthreatening material in an attempt to ease the individual again.

If the suspect *doesn't* exhibit the same mannerism while talking about the weather, it's likely that the gesture is a reliable sign that they are hiding something. The investigator will then utilize the identified behavior for the remainder of the interrogation by looking for a similar reaction. If the tell continues to only be observed during incriminating questions, it's likely to be a sign of deception. It's an unconscious manifestation of guilt. This is also the point in the interview where I'm nodding my head in agreement with the suspect but secretly smiling inside because I know I've got them.

People who are being honest and upfront don't generally exhibit mannerisms or tics when asked about a specific topic. They may feel pressure because they're being questioned, but if they know they did nothing wrong, they will usually look you in the eye and tell you that. Only by comparing their body language during control and pointed questioning can we figure out if the person is being forthright.

Regardless of who you're dealing with—a friend, a family member, an employee, or an employer—using this fact-based approach can assist in making better personal and professional decisions. Determining whether a person is telling the truth or not allows you to skip the bullshit and get right to what really matters: can this person be trusted? Whether you're at the office or at home, understanding the *tells* of the people in your life will help you discern fact from fiction. Be cognizant of what a person is saying, but be even more aware of what their body language is telling you. It's a lot easier to deceive with your mouth than it is with your eyes.

YOUR EYES ALWAYS TELL THE TRUTH

One night I was investigating a complaint about a domestic disturbance. The woman who had answered the door and let me into her apartment appeared to be calm and composed. She was slightly out of breath but did not appear to be nervous or in need of help. Still, it was my job to find out what had happened and whether the suspect who allegedly attacked her was still around.

"Are you okay?" I asked.

"Yes, I'm fine."

"Is your boyfriend still here?"

"No."

She said "no," but when she replied I noticed that she had glanced toward a particular room. Eye movement can be a dead giveaway about whether someone is lying. In this case I did not have time to develop the series of observations that we typically obtain in a police interrogation. My sixth sense was instantly triggered by her body language as she answered my question. She had looked me in the eye the entire conversation until I questioned her about her boyfriend's whereabouts. Her momentary break in eye contact spoke volumes about what she was really thinking. I knew from past experience that people sometimes subconsciously look in the direction of something they're thinking about—in this case, a hidden person. Sure enough, we found the boyfriend hiding in the next room. That room was located in the same direction where her eyes had wandered.

One of the most obvious signals that someone may be lying is when they look away instead of directly at you. If they look you in the eye when they're talking about how the New England Patriots are doing but look away when answering questions about something that may paint them in a negative light, it's a potential sign of deceit.

Another indicator you can pick up on in a person's eye movement relates to memory. Because of the way the brain is wired, some people have a tendency to look left when searching for established memories and right when creating them. I had a few occurrences during my career where I would ask a witness if they had heard gunshots the previous night, and they would look in the direction of their left ear before answering me. This is a natural reaction when a person is searching the logical side of their brain for a sound they might have heard or an image they may have seen.

Neurologists have determined that the right side of the brain is more involved with creativity and imagination. So if a person looks up to the right instead of their left when questioned, it could be an indication that they're *creating* a sound or image rather than searching for one in their memory. Having this knowledge may tip you off to the fact that the next words out of their mouth may not be entirely accurate.

The eyes of a person can be very telling and should be monitored closely, but you also have to keep in mind that it's not uncommon for a person who is just socially awkward to display some form of uncharacteristic eye movement. It pays to know the difference so that you avoid interpreting what is normal for them as a possible indication that they're misleading you. Being equipped with the intuition to decipher the difference between common behavior and signs of deception can help you prevent false assumptions.

The foregoing observations about eye movement are general and clearly shouldn't be the only evidence you rely on to determine whether a person is lying. Although the eyes can be windows to the truth, we shouldn't jump to conclusions based solely upon the evidence of a single mannerism. Nevertheless, it *is* worth carefully noting what a person does with their eyes since, in conjunction with other factors, it can help you determine the person's true intentions. In the case of the woman who was hiding her guilty boyfriend, I used the motion of her eyes, the nature of the crime, and witness testimony to complete my overall assessment. There's a reason many professional poker players wear sunglasses at the table when millions of dollars are on the line, and it's not just to make a fashion statement. Overall, consider eye moment one more tool at your disposal when using your sixth sense.

All the techniques we've discussed can be applied in a variety of situations. I used the observation of body language in the *Big Brother* house to figure out when people were being deceptive on numerous occasions. One day we were sitting at the kitchen table having lunch, and the topic of where we went to school came up. As we discussed the subject, one of my competitors said, "I went to West Point." Then another competitor asked him, "For four years?"

"No. Only two years."

I immediately turned to him.

"No you didn't," I said. "I know you didn't go to West Point."

He put up a weak argument in his own defense, but within sixty seconds, he admitted that he was lying about attending the prestigious military academy.

How did I figure this out so quickly? First of all, I was observing his body language: He avoided eye contact with us and looked at his food as he spoke. He also had a hat on and tucked his head down so the brim of his cap covered his face. These physical signs caught my attention because at this point, I had already become familiar with his normal mannerisms after living with him for a few weeks. In every conversation we had had prior to this, he always looked me directly in the face. He was a confident guy, and this was not his normal behavior. That was the first clue. I also observed his chest movement and could see that he was breathing heavier and faster than usual. This can occasionally be an indication that someone is anxious or nervous. I then focused on his answers to the questions, and his claim that he had attended West Point for two years. West Point is usually a four-year, not a two-year school. Additionally, he had told me a few days earlier that he had been deployed to Iraq while in the military. So that information, coupled with his current age, didn't add up for me.

So his initial body language involving his lack of eye contact and elevated breathing was what caught my attention and warned me of a possible misrepresentation. The actual facts of what he had said were what exposed him. He was too young to have completed basic training, been deployed overseas, and attended a four-year school. Based on the totality of the circumstances, I was able to conclude very quickly that he was being dishonest.

This may sound like an elaborate, drawn-out process, but believe me, it happens fast. This particular incident took under a minute. If you doubt what I'm saying, I encourage you to google it. It's available for everyone to see on YouTube.[12] Got to love the internet.

KNOW *THEIR* ROLE

Work can be a tricky place to navigate, but being aware of who you're working with is always beneficial to your overall performance. It pays to know everyone around you and understand that some of them are going to be valuable, while others…well, let's just say that some will be less than helpful. By using your sixth sense to identify and distinguish between them, you'll improve things for yourself and your organization by utilizing the good and avoiding the bad.

But how do you make that distinction? How do you figure out which colleagues and bosses will be advantageous to you and which will hinder your productivity? I use my sixth sense to classify colleagues into two types of groups, which I refer to as the *opportunists* and the *enthusiasts*. As I describe these two types of people, you'll probably think of a few of your current coworkers who fit into these categories.

The first group I want to talk about are the **opportunists**. They can usually be seen gossiping with other colleagues or supervisors and will look guilty when you walk in on one of their conversations. Try to avoid working with them, but if for some reason you're forced to team up, monitor their actions closely. Be aware of the fact that they're in it more for themselves than for the group. Opportunists are not usually able to get by on their own merit, so they like to associate with people in power. They don't do much work; instead, they befriend their managers to further their *own* career through preferential treatment. To put it bluntly, these individuals are bad for any organization and will only create dissension in the workplace.

Hopefully, with the help of your sixth sense, you'll be able to gravitate toward colleagues who *are* helpful to the organization—the **enthusiasts**. By associating with these people, you're likely to get more done and further the goals of the organization. It's easy to spot enthusiasts: they jump in with both feet to get the job done, and they're supportive of team goals. They work alongside you and help out, no matter what task you're trying to accomplish. They're not ass-kissers, and they don't talk behind your back. Partner up with these supportive people, and you're going to get more done as an individual and as a unit.

In addition to your coworkers, your supervisors can also be classified into various types of leaders. The three most common are *politicians*, *delegators*, and *mentors*.

The leaders I refer to as **politicians** are high-ranking, but they're not really helping the group as much as they're helping themselves, making sure that it's *their* name in the headlines. They don't want to do the hard work; they don't want to be in the trenches with you. But when it comes time for the awards, the accolades, they're at the front of the pack, letting everyone know that the favorable outcome was a result of *their* leadership.

In a corporate setting, let's take the example of a manager who the salespeople never see on the floor. When sales are up, in his mind *he's* the reason it's occurring—even though he's never sold a single thing. He's going to be the one standing in front of his supervisor explaining how *he* achieved this objective.

As you may have noticed, these individuals are similar to opportunists, but they have more power within the organization. Politicians usually won't impede your performance, but they sure won't help you expand your abilities or increase your knowledge. Understand that you can still excel under their interpretation of "leadership," but that they won't be a contributing factor to your success.

Delegators are also high-ranking but not quite at the top yet. Most individuals who fit into this category will be found within middle management. Although they're in charge of certain people, they still have bosses they have to answer to, and there may be times when *they're* assigned specific tasks. They'll say to their supervisor, "I'll get it done for you by next week." But what the delegator actually does is leave that closed-door meeting and find their subordinates. They'll say, "Hey, Derrick, what are you up to?" If you tell them that you're currently working on something, they'll use the all-too-familiar phrase, "When you get a second..." or "When you have the time..." If you've already identified this supervisor using your sixth sense, you'll know what's coming next. "When you have some time, can you complete these accounting sheets? Oh, and by the way, I need them by Friday."

Notice how it conveniently went from, "When you have time" to "I need it by *this date*." It changed from what appeared to be a favor to an assignment with a deadline. And it's obvious that the task they have asked you to perform is something that a manager should be doing, but they don't want to do it. They want *you* to do it for them. They want to be in a position of power, but they don't want to take on the responsibilities that come with the title. They're lazy. They're delegators.

You may think that delegation is a good thing, and it is—in its proper place. If you have a large task that can be divided into smaller assignments, delegation is a good way to operate. An *effective* delegator is a person who wants to see the group succeed and puts everyone in the right position to do the job that they're best suited for. But the *ineffective* delegator that I'm referring to could have one task that they're fully capable of completing on their own but still chooses to pass it along to someone else. They're not bad people, but unfortunately they're looking for the easy way out. They want to sit in their office with the air conditioning on while they shop online or work on their golf swing. These individuals are on their way to becoming politicians, but they don't possess the same level of power yet, so for now, they're going to climb the corporate ladder on the backs of their workers. Once you understand how these people operate and know what to look for, you can avoid them, or at least deal with them quickly so you can get back to what *you* need to do.

In stark contrast to politicians and delegators, **mentors** are the leaders who will tell you to do something, and also guide you along the way. They're not giving direction for the purpose of passing off their own responsibilities. Instead, they want to efficiently carry

CHAPTER SEVEN

||||||||||||||||||||||||||||||||||||||||||||||||||||||

LEAD WITH CONFIDENCE

One night while working patrol, we received a 911 call about a woman screaming for help in the middle of the street. All units immediately responded due to the urgent nature of the situation. When we arrived at the scene, I got out of my cruiser and searched the area but couldn't find her. It was a ghost town. No screaming. No woman. Nothing.

I looked at the other officers who had been searching for the woman as well, but none of them had an answer. She was nowhere to be found.

We were all standing outside of our cruisers trying to figure out what was going on, when suddenly we heard a woman's voice desperately yell, "HELP!" But the cry came from above us. I looked up and saw a woman looking down at me from a small apartment window, which was located above a convenience store. I could see her face and how terrified she was, even though it was dark. We quickly moved closer to the window and I yelled up to her.

"Are you okay?"

Through her crying, she managed to reply. "No, I'm not okay. My boyfriend is drunk and he's beating the shit out of me, but he won't let me leave."

"Okay, hold on," I said. "We're coming right up—"

Her face became even more terrified.

"No, don't!" she said, cutting me off abruptly. "Don't come up here! Please stay away! He has a knife, and if you come in, he'll fucking kill me."

These are the situations that you fear most as a police officer. You have a victim who is in imminent danger, but you can't get to her. And if you try to do something, your actions might result in her being hurt or even killed. Cop or not, that's something no one wants to live with. I was the sergeant in charge that night, and all my officers were looking to me for the next move. I had to make a decision.

I didn't want to risk having the woman get hurt, but I knew we couldn't wait. It was only a matter of time before her boyfriend made his way back to the bedroom she was hiding in and continued his assault. Knowing the suspect was drunk, I thought it might be easy to distract him. Based on that assumption, I had one of the officers go to the back of the building and start flashing his light into a window. I instructed the victim to let me know as soon as her boyfriend went to check out what the light was. The window was at the opposite end of where her bedroom was located, so I thought that would give us the best chance to get to her before her boyfriend did.

The other officers and I quietly made our way up the stairs to the apartment entrance and waited for the victim's cue to break down the door. My guys were itching to get inside, but knowing that the suspect was on the other side of the door with a knife, I told them that I wanted to go first. This was my call, so I wanted to be the recipient of any consequences that came from my decision. If anyone was going to get hurt, it was going to be me.

As soon as I heard the woman yell "He's at the window!" I booted the door and entered the apartment. The suspect was still at the far window looking at the light but immediately turned as we approached him. He was so caught off guard that he didn't have time to make it back to the victim's room. We surrounded him within seconds, and he had no other choice but to drop the knife and put his hands above his head.

The reward? The look of relief on the victim's face when she saw that it was *me* opening her door and not her boyfriend. *That's* why we do what we do.

YOUR TEAM IS YOUR VEHICLE

During my thirteen years in law enforcement, I developed what I believe is a pragmatic approach to management. It may sound exceedingly simple, but that's what you want. Just because something is effective, doesn't mean it has to be overly complicated. Creating a straightforward understanding of your team and the role that each member plays will allow you to recognize the type of supervision they require.

When I looked at the members of my unit, I thought of them as parts of a vehicle, with the vehicle itself representing our team. Some parts are more important than others, but they all contribute to the overall operation of the vehicle. And even though you could run without certain pieces, if you want to run at maximum capability, you need to have all parts in working order.

We know that the various parts of a vehicle are different. Each one has its own purpose and requires its own type of maintenance. An oil change needs to be done every three to five thousand miles, but tires don't have to be changed until you've driven twenty-five to fifty thousand miles. The belts of an engine will have to be monitored as well, but depending on how far you push them, they could last a long time before having to be repaired or replaced.

These examples of the maintenance your vehicle requires can also be applied to the members of your team. You probably have some people who are extremely important to the success of the group. At the same time, you may have other people who are part of the team and contribute to the overall success, but you could still run without them. Some of your team members may need to be checked on regularly, while others can go long periods of time without supervision and their productivity won't suffer. And if you're lucky enough, you'll also have a couple of people whom you don't have to worry about at all. Just check in on them from time to time, making sure they're good, and they'll continue to do their thing.

As a leader, it's your job to decipher who these people are and what part they play. In a police unit, like the one I described earlier in this chapter, all of my guys played a very specific role. One may be breaking down the door, while the other is searching the house. Regardless of what their job is, everyone has to function at the highest level in order to minimize the risk of one us being hurt or killed.

The same mentality can apply to any business environment. Let's take a businesswoman in Miami who runs her own clothing company as an example. She has one main go-getter, another guy who's doing follow-up work, a dozen salespeople, and a few employees who handle clerical and accounting tasks. Every person in her company contributes to how quickly and effectively they can sell and distribute her product. She knows exactly what each person excels at and ensures that their specific role within the organization plays to their strengths. She also knows what type of "maintenance" each person needs in order to remain consistent and productive. Some employees need to be monitored closely, so when they have a large workload, the owner will pay closer attention and increase the amount of communication between them, ensuring that they understand their responsibilities.

She may also have a few employees who need positive reinforcement on a regular basis. If she lets a week or two slide where she doesn't acknowledge them, she'll notice a drop in the quality of their work. With these people, she has to be more hands-on and ensure that she's keeping them accountable. This doesn't mean that they're bad employees, just that they have different needs, and it's her responsibility as a manager to recognize those needs and address them.

In contrast to the employees who constantly need a pat on the back, there are people who don't need supervision at all. The owner will give them a task and they'll finish it the right way and on time. They're self-sufficient, and the only reason she'd need to check in with them would be if an unexpected issue came up. Even in those rare instances, she'll fix the problem, and they'll continue at the same high level of productivity as before.

The vehicle analogy can apply to a variety of situations or professions. Whether it's the whole team or a specific employee, it really doesn't matter. By staying on top of each person and assuring they receive the "maintenance" they need, you'll tend to each part before they break down, creating stability within the organization and avoiding a reduction in the quality of work.

Be proactive in your approach to making sure everyone is working collectively. Think about it this way: Do you want to be on the highway in the middle of nowhere when your car breaks down? Absolutely not. The same philosophy should be applied to your group or organization. You don't want to be in the middle of one of your biggest, most important projects and find out that you have a serious issue within your team. Address potential problems before they occur so that when the big assignment lands on your desk, everyone is at the top of their game and firing on all cylinders.

LEAD BY EXAMPLE

Practice what you preach has always been one of my guiding principles, and it falls perfectly in line with the mind-set of leading by example. I'll admit that it takes courage to stick your neck out and be the first one through the door, but that's what it means to be a good leader. Even in business and in personal ventures, someone has to take the first step. Let it be you.

People learn better when they have an example to follow. It's a human trait that we all share, so when you're working with a team, don't just *tell* them what you want, take the time to *show* them how it's done. Leading by example is one of the most powerful ways to guide a group of individuals toward a common goal. Nothing resonates more with an employee than seeing the boss go out and do exactly what they're asking of them. No words. Just action. You never want to become the "Do as I say, not as I do" guy. If you're passionate about what you do, and you're willing to take calculated risks for the benefit of the organization, your team members will take notice. The hope is that your passion and determination will eventually rub off on them, and before you know it, your team will become a reflection of yourself.

You can see leading by example in full effect with many of the successful college and professional football programs. You'll have a certain type of coach, and whether they're passionate and outspoken or methodical and reserved, the team will take on a similar persona. You know that as a New England guy, I have to bring up the New England Patriots. Coach Bill Belichick is one of the greatest coaches the NFL has ever seen. He is known around the league as one of the hardest working coaches in football, and that dedication to outworking the competition is instilled in all of his players. He believes that everyone on the team, including coaches, has a job to do, and as long as they concentrate on their responsibility, the team will be successful. The entire organization has bought into Belichick's philosophy, and it's not uncommon to see players and coaches wearing the phrase "Do your job" on their clothing or gear. He's also known for taking troubled players and turning them into professionals on and off the field. So how does he do it? He demands excellence by displaying it through his words and actions. He serves as a walking example for his team to follow, letting them know exactly what he expects from them.

The same thing happens within a police department. If a supervisor is passionate about a specific area of law enforcement, such as narcotics or traffic enforcement, the guys under their supervision will usually follow suit and focus on similar aspects of the job. During my career, history taught me that the best drug cops usually come from a shift that was run by a former narcotics detective. There are exceptions, but most of the time the theory holds true: passionate leaders naturally develop equally passionate followers.

Leading by example can also be a very effective practice in the private sector. If you have a guy who's good with numbers and has a gift for accounting, you'll see that his employees will usually pick up similar skill sets and habits. And in many instances, he can accomplish all of this just through his actions. He doesn't have to write anything down, there's no need to create guidelines or policies, and he doesn't have to instill his beliefs through verbal communication. The team will eventually understand what he's trying to do as a result of the way he conducts himself and if they buy into his overall mission, they'll follow along.

One night I was watching one of my favorite shows on television, *Cake Boss*, and a situation came up that really drove home the importance of leading by example. Buddy Valastro is the owner of a successful bakery in Hoboken, New Jersey. In addition to being the owner, Buddy has been a baker since he was a child. Although he still works in the bakery, he usually concentrates on high-priority orders that will appear on the show. In this particular episode, his employees were rolling out a very large piece of pastry dough. We're talking pounds and pounds of dough to make one specific type of pastry. They're very fast, and it's impressive to watch. You can tell that it takes a lot of practice, and it's not something you learn overnight.

One of the newer employees decided it would be a good idea to challenge Buddy and see if he could roll and cut the pastry dough faster than his boss. Buddy gladly accepted the challenge. By the time it was over, you could see that it was close, but Buddy had clearly beaten him. You might expect a winner to gloat, but after he demonstrated his superiority, Buddy was very humble. He basically said to his young employee, "Hey, man, your boss has still got the tools." You could see the employee thinking to himself, and it was probably something along the lines of "Wow, I'll never call him out again." More importantly, Buddy's actions set a precedent for not only that employee, but the rest of the team around him. He didn't take the easy way out and tell them to do it a certain way because that's how he wanted it done. He showed them that the technique they were using was how he's always done it, and if done right, it was also the fastest. In this situation, Buddy not only taught by example; he earned respect.

The message is pretty straightforward: sometimes you have to go out there and put your money where your mouth is. This important principle has the potential to create a heightened level of understanding that can only be accomplished by demonstrating exactly what you expect. One of the greatest basketball coaches of all time, John Wooden, once said, "The most powerful leadership tool you have is your own personal example."[13] Take Coach Wooden's advice and let your actions speak louder than your words.

BUY WHAT YOU'RE SELLING

A few years ago, our police chief surprised us with an updated policy. He wanted us to start wearing our hats during patrol stops. His reasoning was that it looked more professional and signaled to people that we were police officers.

I understood the rationale, but I still didn't like it. Wearing a hat may look good, but it's not practical and can be a distraction. You don't want guys worrying about being seen without their hat on when they should be concentrating on their safety.

Even though I didn't agree with the policy, I explained it to my shift and advised them of the repercussions if they didn't adhere to it. Later that night while we were all in the lunchroom, one of the guys brought it up again.

"Sarge, you can't tell me you agree with the new hat policy, can you?"

Now I could have lied and said, "Yes, of course I do." But I didn't. I wanted to be honest with them.

"Listen, there are going to be things during your career that you have to do that you don't personally agree with. That's part of any job. Do I agree with it? No. But we have to follow the rules. Getting in trouble over a hat isn't worth it." They all looked at me, a few nodded, and that was the end of it.

I advise leaders to follow this basic rule: *buy what you're selling.* I'm talking about believing in what you're saying. The best sales-man is the one who actually believes in his own product. When you're in charge, only push ideas that *you* truly believe in. If it's something you wouldn't do yourself, don't force it on others.

In the hat situation, it was policy, and for that reason alone, it had to be followed. Love it or hate it, that's the way it was, and that's exactly what I told my guys. They respected the fact that I didn't give them some politically correct answer. Instead, I told the truth. The acknowledgment that I agreed with them from a practical standpoint, even though I was going to follow policy, was enough. If I had lied, they would have seen right through me, and it would have created a lack of trust. You can't ruin your credibil-ity just to push someone else's agenda.

Honesty is one of the most important traits in a leader. If you come across as genuine, your people are more likely to trust you. If you abandon honesty because you feel lying can help you get something accomplished, you're playing a dangerous game. The people you lie to may not say it to your face, but they'll remember that you weren't straight up with them in the past. This skepticism will cause them to question everything you say and do. This is not something you want, unless you enjoy explaining every decision you make.

Let's say you tell your team that if they hit their quota, you'll reduce next month's quota by 10 percent in order to give them a break. They believe what you say and work their asses off to hit the mark. If you don't follow through on your promise, trust me, they'll remember. And the next time you really need a push and try to incentivize them with time off or an increase in pay, you probably won't have the same response you did the first time. Bottom line: don't make false promises.

Because of the association between honesty and leadership, it's always advisable to think before you speak. If you don't mean it, don't say it. Plan ahead before giving orders, making sure you're speaking from the heart *and* the mind. Gain the trust and respect of your peers by proving your word is good. When a group of people truly believes in you, it's much easier to lead them.

One school of thought that I don't agree with is the practice of spinning something a certain way in order to have someone buy into it. I'm just not a fan of this approach. I may not share my personal opinions on a specific matter, but I certainly don't give a false impression on how I feel about it either. As I mentioned earlier, that's not the way I'm built, and for the most part, approaching a situation with honesty has worked in my favor. Unless you're playing a game like *Big Brother* or working in an undercover capacity, you really have no excuse, and sooner or later it will catch up with you. Tell it like it is. Incorporating this type of transparency in your life will make it easier to communicate and will help you build stronger relationships.

What I'm proposing is important to parents too. Our children are always observing us, and if you're trying to teach your child something, you better be doing it yourself. While writing this book, I had been accidently swearing around my daughters. I have a terrible mouth, but I'm working on it, I promise. The whole situation started when my oldest daughter said something she shouldn't have. I corrected her and explained how inappropriate it was to use profanity. She took what I said to heart, and now *she's* the one correcting me! Obviously, this is not the way I planned it. And although it's funny to talk about, it's a serious matter. Even though she's not swearing, she sees the whole issue as something I don't take seriously. The solution to this problem is to wrap my head around the idea that as a leader and role model, I have to buy into what I'm selling to her. If I don't believe in it, neither will she.

CHOOSE YOUR BATTLES

If you're fortunate enough to be in a position of power, don't be the person who spreads negativity and has a complaint about everything they don't personally agree with. Pick your battles wisely. In some organizations, you'll find people who will contest every single issue, and it only leads to divisiveness.

We've all seen a supervisor who complains about everything. They basically talk to hear themselves and enjoy stirring the pot. Whether it's a union issue, a personnel issue, or they just don't agree with what someone else is doing, they'll have an opinion and make sure everyone knows it. The sad thing is, in some cases they make valid points. The problem is that they run their mouth so often that when they speak up, everyone automatically tunes them out. They've lost a measure of authority because their words are so diluted by their constant complaining. Everyone knows they couldn't care less about the actual issue, they're just bitching because they like the sound of their own voice.

As a manager, you're creating an environment where the people who look to you for guidance will see your behavior as a socially acceptable practice. Their excuse will be, "Hey, if it's okay for them to do it, it must be okay for me to do it." Establishing an atmosphere where it's reasonable to lodge a complaint, even when there's no merit, will only result in conflict among colleagues.

Leaders who pick and choose their battles and speak up only

when something is actually important to them are much more effective. Develop a reputation for speaking with authority on topics you're knowledgeable and passionate about. This display of poise and patience is what you want your subordinates to emulate. That way, when you *do* decide to speak, because they know it's a rarity for you to do so, your peers will actually listen. *That* is the type of conduct you want to instill in the people you lead.

IMPART PASSION AND INSPIRE COURAGE

I'm passionate about helping others. I became a cop to defend the defenseless, and those around me know how seriously I take that responsibility. In addition to serving the community, I also make a conscious effort to treat everyone with respect, and that includes the people I arrested. Sometimes good people make bad decisions, so you have to keep that in perspective when dealing with someone who may be going through a difficult time in their life. I tried to engrain that same mentality in the officers I was responsible for.

You can always tell which shifts have the new, enthusiastic supervisors looking to make their mark. Their shifts are usually the most active and productive. How does a new supervisor accomplish this? They go out every day and set the tone for others to follow. As I said earlier, it's a common occurrence to see the rest of the officers emulate their supervisor's mentality and approach to the job. And this goes for almost any trade or profession. When the boss's uniform is squared away and they take pride in their work, they expect the same from the people that work under them. If the supervisor is lazy, lacks drive, and doesn't care about their appearance, the people they're responsible for are often going to conduct themselves in a similar manner.

By definition, it's a leader's responsibility to inspire others. You accomplish this fundamental duty by loving what you do and letting others see your enthusiasm. Law enforcement is a proactive profession. I drove around for eight to twelve hours a day, searching side streets, checking buildings, and stopping cars. I truly loved what I did, so I didn't really consider it "work." Don't hesitate to show people that you love your job. Enthusiasm is infectious. Humans have a way of sensing when someone is in a positive frame of mind. They'll see it in your actions, hear it in your voice, and read it in your eyes.

Creating passion for the job amongst your team is instrumental to your success, and you can use that passion to inspire coworkers to be courageous, especially when taking risks. On the streets, courage is a prerequisite. It involves running toward the screams when everyone else is running away. It's staying in the fight when the odds are stacked against you. It's standing up for what's right, even when it's not the popular opinion. Regardless of the situation, remember that courageousness can be spread to those around you. They'll see how you handle adversity, and it will hopefully inspire them to do the same.

The courage and enthusiasm you're promoting can sometimes be drawn from past experience. I regularly led officers into dangerous situations, and that's wasn't something I took lightly. It wasn't only the officers who were depending on me to make the right decision, it was also their family members who expected their loved ones to come home at the end of the shift.

When faced with a difficult decision, I pull from past experiences and their outcomes to determine the right course of action. The more exposure you've had to a similar situation, the more confidence you'll have in your ability to make the right call. Your self-assurance in that moment is what inspires those around you to follow your lead. They may not have the same level of experience as you, but that doesn't matter. Their belief in you is enough to instill the courage needed to do what you ask of them without hesitation.

Although it may not be as dangerous as running down an armed suspect, the private sector also requires a certain level of courage to be successful. Big rewards usually come from taking big risks. Some of the most successful people in the world would not be where they are today if they hadn't risked it all at one point in their life. Take Bill Gates, for example. After two years at Harvard, he dropped out and started Microsoft, and we all know how that turned out. I'm not saying that everyone should drop out of school, but you have to give credit where credit's due. It takes a lot of courage (and balls) to leave one of the most prestigious schools in the country to start your own business.

It's your job as a leader to inspire employees to take those same chances by creating an environment where they're not afraid to fail. Your willingness to take risks with them will show that you believe in their abilities. Think about it this way: if you knew your boss had your back regardless of the outcome, wouldn't you be more willing to take a few calculated risks? Of course you would. You want your employees to be courageous enough to go the extra mile, to be innovative, to take a creative gamble.

History has shown us that being bold can pay off in a big way and has resulted in huge returns on numerous occasions. So promote a culture that embraces self-confidence and courageousness, and you too may be part of something extraordinary.

KNOW YOUR OWN VALUE

Whenever it comes to taking a risk, I've always said that there's no one I'd rather invest in than myself. That's not cockiness, that's confidence. I know what I bring to the table. When I put my mind to something, no one will work harder than me. This mind-set is a winning approach. It's worked for me, and it will work for you too if you really commit to it.

That belief comes from knowing your abilities and the type of work you can produce. I have led men and women into numerous life-threatening situations, and my decisions could have resulted in one of us not going home at the end of the night. When faced with a possible outcome of this severity, you have to be confident in your decision-making abilities and express that through your actions. That's not something you can turn on and off. It's a belief in yourself that must be present at all times, allowing you to respond at a moment's notice without hesitation. You need to trust your discretion and utilize that self-assurance to enhance your effectiveness as a leader. But how do you develop this confidence?

A large part of the answer boils down to drawing from your own training and experience. Knowing that you're both mentally and physically prepared to handle any situation gives you the courage to face the unknown. For me, it's the training I received during the police academy and the experience I gained on the streets of Central Falls, both as a resident and as a cop. Although I haven't seen everything, I've seen enough to know that when my back's against the wall, I'll do what's right. Draw from the moments in *your* life to strengthen the belief in your own judgment. Once you start to carry yourself with confidence, you'll command that same level of respect from others.

My brother is actually a firefighter in Cranston, Rhode Island, but before working for his current department, he was a firefighter in Central Falls. There were a few occasions where I had to watch him enter a house while it was engulfed in flames. Of course I worried about his safety, but I could see in his eyes that he wasn't afraid. He carried himself in a way that told me he was confident in what he was doing, and I could tell by his demeanor that he was going to be okay.

My brother and I have talked about the dangerous situations we've been in and how we were able to keep our composure. We both agreed that it was largely due to our preparation and self-confidence. And the two go hand and hand. The preparation was the extensive training we received prior to the critical incident. The self-confidence came from that same training, knowing that regardless of what was thrown at us, we were ready for it. And when you have a firefighter or a cop who is confident in their decision to enter a burning building or go after an active shooter, their comrades will be right there with them.

On the night we entered the apartment with the battered woman and her knife-wielding boyfriend, I believed in what we were about to do. I'm not denying that I was apprehensive too. I would have been a fool not to be concerned for my own safety, the safety of my men, and the safety of the woman. But you can have more than one feeling at the same time. Although I felt worry and concern, the stronger feeling was confidence. I was convinced that we could get into the apartment and help her before she was harmed. This grace under fire is what people will notice in you. But before they can see it, you have to see it in yourself. You have to know your own value.

In 2012, an Austrian parachutist by the name of Felix Baumgartner jumped from a helium balloon twenty-four miles above New Mexico. He fell so fast on his descent that he broke the sound barrier, the first man to do so without a jet engine. He did the stunt to generate publicity for Red Bull, and in the process, displayed a level of conviction that is hard to even fathom.

Where do you conjure up the intestinal fortitude to do something like that? Did he just randomly decide one day to jump from space? I don't think so. He prepared for it over the course of many years. First he trained in the Austrian military as a parachute jumper. Then he did several test jumps in the United States, specifically to prepare for the Red Bull event. He used all of his previous experience to build up his own self-confidence, allowing him to do something that most wouldn't even attempt.

Of course, no one can deny that some individuals have a natural ability that transcends preparation, but practice and repetition are what build the self-assurance needed to perform under pressure. One of my all-time favorite athletes, Michael Jordan, possessed a high level of self-confidence in his own abilities. There's no getting around the fact that MJ was a natural talent, but he didn't simply rely on that. He was the first one in the gym and the last one to leave. His willingness to constantly improve as a player is the reason why he always wanted the ball when the game was on the line. He wanted to be the one to take the final shot because he knew he would make it. Michael Jordan knew his own value.

We see examples all the time, where natural ability and preparation create a confidence that is vital to success. Although Baumgartner and Jordan were successful in different arenas, what they shared was a profound belief in their own abilities regardless of what others thought. That is what differentiates those who are good from those who are great.

No one is saying that you have to jump from the edge of space or be a fanatic in the gym to fully comprehend what you're capable of. If that were the case, few of us would ever get there. Achieving self-confidence in *your* particular field will naturally depend on what you're specifically trying to accomplish. Whatever education or training is needed to successfully complete your mission, go out there and get it. It's imperative to your performance to stay on top of your game and continue to evolve.

Before I went on *Big Brother,* I told myself that I was going to win. I said the same thing to my close friends and family. I promised them that I would outwork everyone in the competition.

My confidence was derived not only from my prior experiences in law enforcement, but also because I knew what I was playing for. A wife. A daughter. Our future. It was an opportunity to provide a life for them that would otherwise not be possible. I knew going into the house that they would have to kill me to beat me. I know that sounds extreme, but that was my mentality. I wasn't leaving my family for three months for a free vacation to California. My belief in myself and my determination to win for my family was all I needed to stay focused on the mission. So when my wife asked me, "Why are you doing this?" my response was simple: "Because I'm going to win." I knew my value. My hope is that *this* book will do the same for you because knowing your own value creates confidence—the same confidence needed to lead.

UNDERSTAND YOUR ASSETS

When we hear the word "leader," we often think of a single individual, and that's true, to a certain extent. But there's a big difference between being a leader and being an *effective* leader.

At the time of writing this book, I had been hearing a lot about who President Trump had selected to be part of his cabinet. There is always a lot of interest around the president's picks because everyone knows how significant of a role these people play in the president's ability to lead.

Part of picking the right individuals involves knowing what each person specializes in, allowing them to utilize their skills to benefit the current objective.

When I was a member of the special investigations unit, we

executed many narcotics search warrants. I don't care how tough you are, running into a house when you don't know what's waiting for you is unnerving. Fortunately, I was never alone. There were always at least three other officers to assist with the operation. Was I still anxious about what we might encounter? Of course. But was I confident? Absolutely. Although I knew the risks we faced, I also knew the people I was with. These guys were well versed in their jobs, and they all had specific tasks based on their abilities: one guy was in charge of breaking down the door; one guy was responsible for apprehending the main suspect; and the other guys would concentrate on clearing the rest of the house. Their assignments were not given at random. Each individual was designated the job that I knew they were best suited to handle. Knowing who they were, what they excelled at, and how to use them is what gave me the confidence to lead them.

We've all seen a police officer in their element. At any moment they may have to give an order—to an oncoming vehicle, to a fleeing suspect, or to an individual with a gun who's refusing to drop it. Most people would consider this extreme, but for a cop, it's just another day at work.

Although the above scenarios dictate a level of authority, barking orders won't be the best option in most situations. Yes, there has to be a level of self-assurance in your voice when assigning responsibilities, but your colleagues have to believe in *you* before doing what you've asked. Knowing who you're talking to and the best way to lead them will give you the confidence to delegate with conviction, leaving your team wondering not *if* but *when* they'll accomplish their mission.

CHAPTER EIGHT

||||||||||||||||||||||||||||||||||||||||||||||||||||||||

USE YOUR HEAD

I'm a firm believer in the idea that regardless of your natural ability, the more you do something, the better you'll get at it. Everyone's heard the phrase *Practice makes perfect*, but how many people actually take the time to follow this advice? It takes dedication to get off the couch and put in the daily work that's required to progress. Some people just don't have the drive or determination for it. But what if I told you there's another way to gain the benefits of practicing without having to exhaust any *physical* effort? That you could rehearse certain goals anytime you wanted to without leaving your own home? Would you be more likely to commit to this form of self-improvement? I believe that most people would. And although there's no true replacement for physical practice, *visualization* techniques can serve as an effective alternative. The best way to enhance your abilities is through repetition, and mental preparation gives you the advantage of repeatedly performing a function without exerting any physical energy.

Visualization techniques can increase performance in almost any setting. Giving a presentation at work or at school. Preparing for an interview. Getting ready for a sporting event. These are just a few of the scenarios that most people would prefer to practice ahead of time but are unable to replicate. Although there may be some limitations— say, your current environment or lack of the necessary equipment— that shouldn't stop you from *mentally* preparing for what you'll be facing. Envisioning a set of circumstances that are consistent with the physical actions you'll be performing may sound unconventional, but it can dramatically increase your chances of success.

I started using visualization techniques when I was still in high school playing baseball. I continued that practice all through college and into my career as a police officer. I can't tell you how many times I mentally prepared for an interrogation while I was in the bathroom. I know that might sound a little weird, but let's be honest, that's where most of us do our best thinking. I would run through all of my questions and what their responses might be in my head. When it came time to actually sit down with the individual, I had a heightened level of confidence because the situation felt familiar, even though I had never met them before.

When I applied for *Big Brother*, I remember imagining my first call with the casting agency. I thought about Robyn Kass, the casting director, introducing herself and explaining that she was considering me for the show. I tried to place myself in the same emotional state that I would be in after hearing something like that. I ran through the different questions she might ask and answered them as if I were actually on the phone with her. By repeatedly running through that scenario, it prepared me for anything she could possibly throw at me. When the call finally came, I was ready.

The people who are the best at what they do are the ones who put in the work to maintain, if not improve their abilities. Athletes, performers, and speakers—these are all jobs that can be considered intimidating, but to those who are successful in these fields, it's second nature. Why is that? Is it because they're better than you? No. Are they smarter than you? Not necessarily. It's because they do it all the time, and you don't. They have confidence in themselves and what they're doing because they're comfortable in that setting. But how did they reach that point? Regardless of natural ability, when you do something for the first time, it's to be expected that your performance might be rough around the edges. But when you perform an action on a consistent basis, you learn what works and what doesn't. So, the question becomes: How do you gain that all-important self-assurance without having to go through the physical repetition? This question is especially vital for unfamiliar tasks that you're going to be tackling for the first time.

Whenever we take on a new endeavor, there has to be a first attempt. Do you want your first time to be when it really counts, or would you rather be in a situation where you can practice and make adjustments? I think most of us would choose the latter. I know some people like to jump right in without any preparation, but why gamble when you can have a guarantee?

By mentally preparing for an assignment, you can make mistakes without the fear of failure. You can take steps to counteract any errors you encounter along the way. The beauty of mental preparation is that you can perfect your performance *without ever actually performing.* Just because you've never *physically* done something before doesn't mean you still can't *mentally* experience it. You have within you the ability to put yourself into any scenario and attempt any task, just by using your imagination.

Visualization is not only an asset when it comes preparation; it's also advantageous on the road to self-improvement. The mind is a powerful thing, and studies have shown that by repeatedly thinking of an action, you can improve your abilities almost as much as those who physically practice.[14] Let that sink in for a second. You can actually get better at something just by going through the motions in your head. Sound easy? Well, it is. And you don't even have to be awake to do it. Many people, including myself, do a lot of productive thinking while they're asleep. For years, I kept a notepad by my bed so I could write down any ideas that came to me throughout the night, but now I just use my iPhone. We all have to sleep, and there are many benefits to doing so. Why not add one more?

Whatever you currently do to get ready for a personal mission, keep doing it, but add in some mental preparation, and then evaluate its effectiveness on your execution. You have nothing to lose and everything to gain. I think you'll be impressed with the impact mental rehearsal can have on your overall performance. Don't underestimate the power of visualization; embrace it. Make it the X factor of your success.

MENTAL REHEARSAL

I read an article a few years ago about the benefits of mentally rehearsing an action before attempting it. Researchers at the University of Chicago divided subjects into three groups.[15] The individuals in each group were tested to see how well they were able to shoot a free throw. After the results were recorded, each group was given specific instructions. One group was allowed to practice free throws for an hour each day. The second group was not allowed to practice at all. And the third group was put into a room for an hour each day and instructed to only *think* about shooting a free throw.

After thirty days, the researchers brought each group back in to be retested, and for me, the results were completely unexpected. Those who were not allowed to practice in any way had no improvement, which wasn't really a surprise. The group that had practiced for an hour each day had an improvement of 24 percent. Again, I expected that. What was shocking to me was that the group who only used visualization techniques as a form of practice had a 23 percent improvement rate. Yes, you're reading that right. There was only a 1 percent difference between the people who physically practiced and the ones who mentally prepared. Without lifting a finger, the individuals who only used mental rehearsal scored almost as high as the subjects who actually shot the basketball!

The researchers concluded that although two of the groups did very well, *the optimal form of preparation was a combination of both physical and mental rehearsal.* This understanding is the key to positive results in many situations, from sports to interpersonal interactions, from public speaking to a job interview. What we can take from this is that with any of these challenges—and many others— mental visualization *will* improve your overall performance.

Now, I'm not saying it's okay to sit on your ass and do nothing all day. What I am saying is that if you can have this much improvement just by mentally rehearsing, imagine the possibilities if you incorporate this practice in conjunction with physical repetition. There's really no downside to hedging your bets when it comes to the best approach for success, so why not take full advantage of both forms of preparation?

When I talk about visualization, I'm *not* talking about daydreaming. They're two completely different things. When you daydream or fantasize, you envision more of an overview of what you would like to accomplish in the future. There's no substance to it. You paint an overall picture but avoid the details required to reach it. You skip over the hard stuff and get right to the reward. Now, there's nothing wrong with that. It's actually a good thing. It motivates you to work harder, but it still doesn't cover the small, necessary tasks.

On the other hand, when you make a conscious effort to visualize something, you're going through that assignment or function as if it's actually happening. You're not merely thinking about the results; you're mentally rehearsing the entire process leading up to them. It's still okay to think about success and what comes with it, but that's not what makes visualization techniques beneficial. What's important to mental rehearsal are all the minor details that surround whatever you want to do, and you must repeatedly visualize all components of that function for the process to work.

When the volunteers in the basketball experiment were put into isolation for an hour, they were instructed to visualize every element of a free throw: stepping up to the line, the feel of the basketball in their hands, its weight and texture, and then the motion of raising the ball up over their head and letting it go. They would envision the ball leaving their hands and then going through the net as they completed their follow-through. They didn't need to be on the court to improve their game. In the end, mental rehearsal, with all the accompanying sensory details, was their X factor. And it can be yours too.

Let's say you have to put on a presentation at school or at work, but public speaking really isn't your thing. It would be a good idea to run the scenario through your head a few times before actually doing it. I know that some people would prefer to write something up and just go for it, and that's fine. More than likely, that would be sufficient, and I know that students and professionals get away with that approach all the time. I've even had to do it on a few occasions myself. But will that performance represent your best work? Will it showcase what you're really capable of?

A lot of people would say, "Hey, I have kids to take care of." Or "I had three other assignments on top of that one."

This is exactly why visualization is so convenient. You can do it for as much or as little time as you want, and it's done at *your* leisure. Ideally, physically performing the assignment in front of your friends or family is the preferable method, but you might not have the time or feel comfortable enough to do so. The advantage of mental rehearsal is that you can still simulate that same experience *without* having anyone in the room—but you have to fully embrace the idea and allow your mind to take the wheel.

Now, you're sitting there saying, "Okay, Derrick, how do I do it?" If you're a student and you know you have to give a presentation in front of your class, you can break down your visualization step by step.

The Set-Up:

- Think about the exact lecture hall that you're going to be in during your speech.
- Picture what you'll be wearing for the presentation.
- Estimate how many students are going to be there and where they might sit.
- Envision yourself being introduced to the class and walking up to the podium.

The Presentation:

- Make sure you say every single word of your speech in your head as you go through the motions. (If you skip over lines in your head to expedite the process, you run the risk of skipping them when you're actually presenting.)

- Go over every piece of content you want to cover throughout the course of the presentation.
- Think about the hand gestures you want to make as you point out certain examples.
- Focus on making eye contact and moving throughout the classroom to hold the audience's attention.

Visualize the situation in its entirety and in as much detail as possible. The sights. The sounds. The smells. Everything.

Place yourself in a virtual reality, where you're literally delivering the presentation at that very moment. The best part about mental rehearsal is that you can repeat the process as many times as you want and the audience will *never* judge you. They'll sit there and listen until *you* decide that you're ready for the real thing.

On a show like *Big Brother*, privacy was a commodity, but that didn't stop me from mentally preparing myself for what I needed to do. I spent a lot of time sitting quietly, staring off into space. Even though it sometimes looked like I was bored or upset, I was actually using mental rehearsal to plan out my next move. I was visualizing all the details of speaking with someone, including what they looked like, how they spoke, and where the conversation would take place. I imagined the things they might say and how I would counter any points they made. I rehearsed the entire conversation and ended it with me winning the exchange. That sense of accomplishment is vitally important to the process because it carries over to the actual event.

When it finally came time to talk with the person, I was confident that I would ultimately get what I wanted. By going into a situation and feeling like you've already seen the outcome, it gives you a distinct advantage. It's like going into a test and having all the answers.

So when and where are the best times and places to practice visualization techniques? The short answer is…anytime and anywhere. It does help, however, if you can integrate some form of mental practice the day before or the day of the event. Even when you're short on time or unable to find an empty space, there's always opportunity to mentally rehearse what you're preparing to do. In the car, in your room, sitting on a couch—it really doesn't matter. Sure, the more private the area, the more you can lose yourself and get into it, but a quiet space is not a prerequisite. I've even rehearsed some speeches while in the shower! One time I actually heard clapping after giving my "speech" and thought I was going crazy, but then I realized it was just my wife making fun of me from the other room. Hey, I can't say she wasn't supportive, right?

Even though you put in the effort to prepare, I'm not saying that when it comes time to step up to the plate, you still won't have a slight feeling of uncertainty. Taking on new challenges can be scary, but in some ways that's a good thing. If you want to improve yourself as a person, you have to be willing to push your comfort zone. However, mentally rehearsing your goals will leave you significantly more poised, reducing your reservations.

When we have a mission, especially an important one, we owe it to ourselves to give our best effort, and mental rehearsal should always be a part of that.

If you had the ability to see into the future, would you do it? I'll say this: until the time machine is invented, visualization is the closest thing you've got, so use it.

PUT YOUR MIND TO WORK

One of my first experiences using visualization as a tool came during my senior year of high school with the arrival of a new baseball coach. I had been in a hitting slump at the plate for the past few games, and I was trying to find a way to break out of it. Before batting, my normal routine was to focus on my timing by watching the pitcher and swinging as if he were throwing to me. This was something that I had been doing since I was in Little League, and it had always worked. The new coach was okay with me continuing to do what I had always done, but he also wanted me to try something new while I was on deck. In addition to working on timing, he suggested that I close my eyes and visualize myself in the batter's box. He wanted me to think about digging my feet into the dirt, adjusting my grip on the bat, and getting ready for the pitch. I had to envision the current pitcher on the mound, replicating his throwing motion, while also thinking about the different pitches he might throw.

Taking the coach's advice, during the next game I stepped into the on-deck circle, got into my batting stance, and closed my eyes. I began by envisioning a fastball coming out of the pitcher's hand, and when it reached me, I visualized myself swinging the bat and making solid contact with the ball, causing it fly to the area of the field I was aiming for. Within a minute or two, I had visualized every pitch at the pitcher's disposal and I knew what to do with whatever he decided to throw at me. By the time it was my turn to bat, I was more confident and composed. I felt like I had already faced him before. Maybe it was a coincidence, but it worked. I started to put the ball in play.

The coach's suggestion also served as a form of meditation, and it helped me to relax before stepping up to the plate. I even started to visualize what I would do before pitching—envisioning myself throwing with good form and painting the corners of the plate with every pitch. After seeing the success I was having with visualization, I knew it was something I wanted to incorporate in every facet of my life…and that's exactly what I did.

At the police academy, I successfully used visualization

techniques to save my ass during the shooting portion of our training. We had a lot of guys who were former military, and here I was, twenty years old, straight out of college, having never shot a gun. Initially, I thought it would be easy. I was definitely that guy who went into it thinking, "It looks easy on TV." Yeah, you guessed it—TV sometimes lies, and I found that out the hard way.

As you can imagine, the qualification course is very difficult—as it should be. They teach you very early on that you're responsible for every bullet you shoot. So even though you hit the target on the third shot, it's equally important where the two rounds that missed end up. We had gone through a couple of practice qualifications leading up to the actual test, and sometimes I would pass, and sometimes I would barely miss the minimum score. When your whole career depends on passing, those aren't the results you want.

I mentally rehearsed every night leading up to the test. I went through the course in my mind as if I were actually there. I would picture holes appearing in the center of the target each time I pulled the trigger. When I was done, I thought about how gratifying it would feel to have the instructor inspect my target and then write across the top of it with a red marker. As a result of my relentless rehearsing, I experienced a familiar sense of calm going into the qualification. It was the same feeling I had every time I stepped into the batter's box. Right then and there, I knew I was ready.

A few days later it was time to take the test. After firing my last shot and having my target inspected, I saw the red four-letter word that I had imagined every day—PASS. *That's* how you use the power of mental preparation to your advantage.

After spending so much time learning how to use a firearm, I decided to take a position in law enforcement that required me to leave my gun at home! Go figure…

Working as an undercover detective is a whole different animal. There's really no universal way to prepare for an undercover operation. But from my experience, there are definitely things that every undercover agent should go over before carrying out an assignment: What's the mission, who's the target, what's the layout, and where will the surveillance team be? This is all standard, and our policies and procedures actually require us to review these variables prior to starting the investigation. But there's also the psychological aspect of preparing for an undercover case, and there's no policy or procedure for that. Everyone has a different way of putting themselves in the right mind-set before doing something that poses such a high risk to their safety. My preparation always consisted of at least a few minutes of visualizing the mission I was about to attempt.

I remember working a drug case for a neighboring agency, and the mission was to infiltrate a group of friends and buy product from a local drug dealer. The target of the case was very apprehensive about new customers and only sold directly to the people he trusted. We also knew that he liked to complete his transactions while in a moving vehicle, but if he had any suspicion that he was being tailed, he would kick the person out of his car immediately. I would have to be in a car with him without backup, so if things went wrong, I would be in a moving vehicle, on my own, with no firearm. I don't care how badass you think you are, that's not an ideal situation.

Prior to meeting the dealer, I already knew what he looked like, how his voice sounded, what kind of car he drove, and the route he usually followed during his transactions. That information allowed me to visualize myself in the car with him before we even met.

Where would I sit to put myself in the best position to see everything around me? How would I make sure that the doors were left unlocked without him noticing? What was I going to say if he started asking certain questions? What if there were other people in the car with us? These were just some of the questions we didn't have answers to, so all I could do was visualize each situation and plan out how I would react. If I didn't like how I handled the situation in my head, I'd run through it again. I did this for every possible scenario I could think of. I wanted to make sure that no matter what predicament, I had an answer for it.

I eventually met up with the target and, as expected, he wanted to make the deal in his car while driving. Unexpectedly, he had a passenger, so I chose to sit in the back seat directly behind him. But where I sat was no coincidence; I had anticipated the possibility of a second person and knew exactly how I wanted to handle it. From where I was sitting, I could still see the dealer's hands and keep an eye on the passenger at the same time. There were no other surprises, we made the deal, and I was able to get out there without putting myself or anyone else in danger. This went on for several weeks as I slowly gained the target's trust.

Eventually, he was arrested and charged for his crimes, and I credit a large part of how smoothly the case went to the intelligence we gathered prior to carrying out the investigation. A lot of manpower and planning went into the surveillance portion of the case, and we gained detailed information about the suspect before I even met him. That intelligence enabled us to anticipate the dealer's next move and allowed me to mentally prepare for who I was dealing with and what I had to do to complete the mission.

The power of visualization isn't magic, even though it can feel that way sometimes. I mean, when you start to think that the mind can affect the real world, it does sound a little supernatural. But the truth is there's a perfectly valid explanation for why mental rehearsal works so well. It all comes down to tricking your subconscious into believing whatever you conjure up in your mind. As Napoleon Hill, author of *Think and Grow Rich*, put it, "Whatever the mind of man can conceive and believe, it can achieve." If you can see something clearly and distinctly in your mind, with so much detail that you can almost feel it, then you can obtain it—regardless of how unlikely it may seem.

SLEEP IT OFF

The process of visualization has many benefits, and I've been preaching throughout this entire chapter that you should use it whenever you can. So it only makes sense that if you're going to use it while you're awake, you might as well use it while you're asleep too. When we retire for the evening, our mind goes through a process of reviewing the things that happened during the day. These events often affect our dreams in one way or another. This natural process of mental review while sleeping provides an unintended benefit for people who want to learn new material and improve their abilities.

The reason many students study for an exam late at night is because they usually put it off until the last minute. I know this because I was one of them. I didn't know it at the time, but I was actually studying when my mind was most likely to absorb new material. As soon as I would doze off, my subconscious would review the data, encoding it into memory. The next day it would be fresh in my mind and ready to be recalled for the examination.

In order to take advantage of mental rehearsal when you're asleep, there are two things you need to do differently. First, you need to review the material you want to learn relatively close to the time you go to bed. This way, the last thing that's on your mind before your head hits the pillow is exactly what you want to work on. The second thing is, as soon as you wake up, review what you thought about while you slept, making notes in your head, in a notebook, or on your phone.[16]

If you're considering implementing visualization techniques into your sleep, it's pivotal that you understand how emotions can interfere with successful mental rehearsal. If the mind is overstimulated by strong emotions, sleep can be hindered. This is why it's best not to think about stressful situations prior to sleep, such as a breakup, financial problems, or something upsetting that you may have experienced during the day. Clear your head before you go to sleep so you can focus on what's important. If you're going to spend time dwelling on a specific subject, make it something positive.

It should come as no surprise that I've used mental rehearsal throughout the process of writing this book. The fact that you're reading my words is proof that positive thinking and mental preparation can have a dramatic impact on motivation and productivity.

I've been imagining this book for over a year now, and to finally have it in front of you gives me a feeling of accomplishment that I've only experienced a few times in my life. But it wasn't always smooth sailing. There were many days when I couldn't find the drive to open my laptop and start banging keys. Like many writers, I had some serious cases of writer's block, and even when the words were flowing, there were many internal battles. No one is more critical of my work than me. I have no problem admitting that there were points during this process when I would delete an entire chapter the day after writing it. I wanted this book to really help people, and the minute I felt that my writing wasn't conveying my message, I would hit the delete button.

Writing a book under this type of internal scrutiny can make for a very long and drawn-out process. And although I spent a significant amount of time writing and revising this manuscript, I spent an equal amount of time imagining the finished product. When I found myself in a rut, I would spend time thinking about what the book would look like and how gratifying it would feel to finally receive my first box of author's copies. To hold the actual book in my hands while reflecting back on some of the trying times during the writing process—that was a feeling I wanted to experience. The only way I would get there was by knuckling down and fighting through the struggle. I didn't want to go out drinking with friends. And I had no urge to spend money on things I didn't need. That type of behavior would only serve as a distraction, not a solution. All it took was a little time to myself to refocus and visualize the overall mission. *That* was all the motivation I needed.

If you make a conscious effort to integrate the same mentality into *your* daily approach, I have no doubt that you'll see similar results—and who knows? I may be reading *your* book someday.

Visualization is a power tool, but it works both ways. If you envision negative outcomes, you're likely to have negative results. How many times have you tried something new, and the minute you started thinking about the one thing you *didn't* want to happen, it did? This is why it's important to refrain from focusing on pessimistic thoughts. If you find yourself dwelling on a less-than-positive outcome, distract yourself with something, anything, and get your mind back on track. When I first started learning how to snowboard, all I wanted to do was make it down the mountain one time without falling. I would start off okay, but as soon as I felt like I was almost at the bottom, I would picture myself falling, and within seconds I would be flat on my back. Instead of concentrating on what was in front of me, I focused on failure.

Negative thoughts can manifest just as easily as positive thoughts. As soon as you devote any attention to the possibility of losing, you've already lost. This is why it's so imperative to stay in the mind-set of positive thinking.

When you visualize what you want to do in life, don't waste your time thinking about what could go wrong—focus on what *will* go right.

CHAPTER NINE

TURN POLICE TACTICS INTO CORPORATE STRATEGIES

It's four o'clock in the morning and still dark outside. Most people are asleep. Down the road from a single-family residence, a white van sits parked on the side of the road with the engine off. Its windows are tinted, so you can't see inside, but if you could, you would see five men sitting in silence. Those five individuals are more alert and awake than most people will be throughout the entirety of their day.

I'm one of the men in that van, and while we're waiting, we're all making our final preparations. Some of us are checking that our rifles are loaded and in the proper fire setting. Others are ensuring that their bulletproof vests are securely fastened, and some of us are just sitting there, thinking about what we're about to do and our loved ones at home, knowing that the outcome may determine whether we see them again.

Regardless of what we're doing separately, we all have one goal in mind: to keep each other safe and accomplish the mission. Once we're given the cue from the lookout that the target house is clear, we exit our vehicle, move into a stack formation, and head toward the house. We stay close together and run in unison. As we approach the building, one man opens the screen door to give the second man a clear shot at the steel door behind it. The second officer carries the battering ram up a small set of stairs and prepares to hit the door. He has been training for this day and knows exactly how hard he needs to swing it. He strikes just below the doorknob with everything he has, taking the door right off its hinges on the first attempt. We then enter the house and break off from each other as we clear each room.

We are on high alert because of the danger we face inside. Without delay, we tactically search the entire residence with our firearms drawn, yelling commands, letting everyone know that the police are there. Within minutes, all targets of the search warrant are in handcuffs.

Fortunately, nobody was hurt, and none of the suspects were able to reach their weapons in time. And thank God for that because if they had, it could've gotten ugly for all of us.

This whole operation took less than five minutes to carry

out, but if it weren't for months of preparation and team management, it wouldn't have gone as smoothly. The coordination and trust it takes to conduct a high-risk assignment like this are not developed overnight. Our successful execution was due to positive team building, group cohesion, and camaraderie, which I'd like to believe was the result of good leadership. These individuals weren't motivated by money or recognition. For them, it was a sense of pride in what they were doing and their desire to make sure that everyone remained safe. This example of a coordinated effort may sound dramatic, but the principles that govern its execution apply to any management situation.

I used to work for a car dealership when I was still in high school. I often stopped in to visit with one of the sales managers because I had a personal interest in learning more about what he did. One morning, I walked in on him and his team while they were in the conference room preparing for a meeting. They were getting ready to pitch a big advertisement proposal for the entire northeast region to the top executives. When the sales manager and his team went into that meeting, they were looking to perform at their highest ability. They all had specific tasks and responsibilities that they had worked on not only that morning, but for months in advance.

After their meeting with the top brass, the sales manager introduced me to the rest of his team and invited me to join them for lunch. While we were sitting in the restaurant, these men and women all had what appeared to be a great connection. They were telling jokes, talking about their children, and making plans for the weekend. I didn't realize it at the time, but this friendly get-together was not only a social gathering; I was in the middle of a team-building session. Even though the team members weren't talking about their jobs, this group lunch was about more than free food; it was about building strong personal relationships, which directly affects productivity in the workplace.

I can't prove it, but I have a strong suspicion the sales manager knew exactly what he was doing. I could tell that these lunches were a common occurrence, and as it turned out, this particular lunch was to celebrate the approval of the advertisement proposal they had just pitched—giving greater credence to the power of team-building and preparation. These informal interactions were part of what made them stronger as a unit, and I think the manager knew that.

Under his leadership, he had done two things to increase the team's chances of success: he delegated tasks that each individual would excel at due to their own personal attributes, and he got the group together on a regular basis to socialize and build relationships that would carry over outside of work.

There was clearly a correlation between their success and the camaraderie I saw around that restaurant table. Both were indicative of strong leadership, which was ultimately the responsibility of one man...their sales manager.

WORKING WITH GROUPS

In any profession, being able to work independently is a valuable asset. But let's face it, when you're trying to accomplish a large task, it usually takes more than one person. Whether it's in an office with five employees or in a global operation with a massive workforce, you'll need people with different backgrounds, capabilities, and skill sets to get the job done.

When I was still assigned to the special investigations unit, we were conducting a large-scale undercover operation involving a confidential informant (CI). The operation was called "Ridin' Dirty," and yes, I named it after a song that was popular on the radio at the time.

The CI would go around to different streets within the city and walk up to the people who we believed were selling narcotics. They would create some type of dialogue and then attempt to complete a hand-to-hand transaction involving the exchange of narcotics for money.

We were surprised to learn that the majority of these dealers were not actually from our city but were attempting to sell their product here. This required us to widen our operation and seek the cooperation of police departments from different jurisdictions.

By sitting down with these other agencies and having multiple meetings with them, we were able to work together, resulting in the arrests of twenty-two suspects. We carried out the entire operation without anyone being hurt or exposing the CI's identity. The operation was ultimately deemed a complete success and received a lot of media attention. More importantly, it built relationships between multiple agencies, which still exist to this day. The point is that no single person could have conducted this entire investigation alone. In order for the operation to be as successful as it was, there needed to be a collaborative effort.

If you want to accomplish the big goals, complete the big tasks, and make the big money, you have to be able to work with others—even if you're temperamentally introverted or downright antisocial. At the end of the day, the smaller tasks can be accomplished by yourself, but when you undertake the more complex assignments, it's going to take a coordinated group effort to get the job done.

SOLVING GROUP CONFLICT

When you're training to be an officer in the police academy, one of the key things you learn is how to evaluate conflicting stories and diffuse hostile situations. Instructors referred to this practice as "verbal judo," and it's something that should be covered in any college-level management program. In my experience, the ability to solve group conflict is one of the most useful tools a manager can possess. The techniques we use in law enforcement to mediate a situation could assist any supervisor in solving a problem between multiple individuals.

When I first became a supervisor, we had an incident where two young women claimed that their "friend" had run a guy over with his truck and then fled the area. What would you do in this situation? How would you determine what really happened? How would you find their friend? Most people would probably continue to interview the girls together in an attempt to learn his identity, but that would be a mistake. These two girls were friends, and by interviewing them at the same time, in the same room, I'd be creating an opportunity for them to alter their stories as they play off of each other. They could tell the same lies and hide the truth by corroborating each other's statements.

Once I had the girls in two different rooms, I let them know right from the start that I wanted to get to the bottom of the story. The first girl claimed that the guy who fled the area was the other girl's boyfriend. But when I spoke with the second girl, she said he was her cousin. There were other discrepancies in their accounts of what had happened, but their conflicting statements about their relationship with the driver was the clearest indication that one of them was lying. The first girl claimed that the guy in the truck was driving in reverse and didn't see the person behind him, causing him to accidentally run the victim over. As I kept going back and forth between the two girls, their statements repeatedly contradicted each other, and when I called them out on it, they didn't have a response.

After about an hour, as I kept pushing the questioning and calling them out on their lies, their stories began to match up—even though they hadn't spoken to each other since being separated. I wore them down mentally, and eventually I was able to figure out what had actually happened. There had been an argument over one of the girls, and the suspect got into his truck and deliberately ran over the victim. So just like that, we went from a hit-and-run to an attempted murder. All because I knew enough to separate the involved parties and question them independently, allowing me to cross-reference their accounts until I figured out the *real* story.

What's important to take from this example is that when you run into a conflict involving multiple people, your best strategy to get to the root of the issue is to draw out the opinions of each person as an individual, not as a group. By doing this, you'll avoid being deceived by the typical collaboration and story fabrication that often takes place when people choose a side before even speaking with you.

You don't need to have a murder case to utilize this approach. It can be an issue between coworkers, family members, or even friends. A friend of mine, who is a teacher, used this same technique when he suspected a student of plagiarizing his essay in a writing class. The student had a close friend in the class who was an A student, but the one who was suspected of cheating was a C student. My friend was under the impression that the underperforming student had asked his friend to write his essay. But instead of confronting them both at the same time, he talked with them separately after class. He began with the A student, complimenting him on his writing ability and telling him how impressed he was with his work. He then pointed out that his friend had not performed as well on his past assignments. However, his latest essay did not contain any of the errors that had plagued his (the friend's) earlier essays, such as awkward writing, fragments, and incorrect use of punctuation. Instead, the essay was perfectly written and was similar in style to how the A student would normally write.

"It could only have been written by you," the teacher said. The young man turned red when confronted with this statement. He knew it was a compliment and an accusation at the same time. Interestingly, he wanted the recognition more than he feared the repercussions, and he admitted the truth. The teacher then interviewed the other student by himself, the one who he now knew had cheated. At first he denied that he had asked his friend to write the essay and even became angry when he was accused of plagiarism. But when confronted with his friend's confession, he had no choice but to also admit to the infraction. If the students had the chance to collaborate on their accounts before speaking with the teacher, they might have actually stuck with their original story. By separating the two young men, the teacher was able to confirm what he already knew.

Pull out the key components that are mentioned by all parties involved, and use those facts as your baseline to develop an understanding of what occurred. Once the stories start to match up, you'll know what the actual conflict is about and can then turn your attention to solving it.

Side note for all the parents out there: this method is also effective when dealing with kids. When they're giving you a hard time and playing the blame game, give it a shot. You can thank me later.

REWARDING POSITIVE BEHAVIOR

Who doesn't like being recognized for doing a good job? With my officers, I have numerous ways of giving them positive feedback. One of the most commonly used means of recognition is a database called the Guardian Tracking System, which allows me to enter positive comments about each officer. The acknowledgment could be for something as simple as helping an elderly woman with her groceries or as serious as saving a person's life. Officers can see these positive comments in the privacy of their homes, and it's a nice way to reinforce their good work without embarrassing them in front of everyone. Some people don't like to have the spotlight on them, and in a police department, guys tend to bust the chops of the officers who are constantly being recognized for their efforts. Although they're kidding around, it can actually cause some officers to reduce their productivity. You always want your employees or team members to associate positive behavior with a positive experience.

Everyone likes to hear that the good work they're doing hasn't gone unnoticed. It makes people feel good about themselves and motivates them to work harder for you. And don't just take my word for it. Psychologists have demonstrated for many years that rewarding positive behavior increases productivity. The Russian physiologist Ivan Pavlov began this research with dogs.[17] American psychologist B. F. Skinner continued this work with pigeons and, ultimately, humans. These researchers discovered the psychological principle known as positive reinforcement, essentially saying behavior that is rewarded will continue or increase.[18] So if it's good enough for these experts, it's good enough for me.

One other point: Skinner and others discovered that reinforcement works best if it's sporadic. You don't reward a positive action every single time it occurs. As counterintuitive as that may sound, it's more effective to reward good behavior intermittently. This will keep positive recognition a rare but desired occurrence, rather than a redundant, almost expected, reward. It also makes recognition more meaningful to the recipient and to those looking to receive similar praise in the future.

Medals, trophies, plaques, and citations all have their place. But sometimes, positive reinforcement can be as simple as saying "Good job!" It's never a bad thing to tell somebody you appreciate what they do. I don't care if you're in the military, in law enforcement, or on Wall Street, it's always good to hear, "Hey, nice work! Keep it up." It may seem like a minor thing, but the two seconds it took for you to give that acknowledgment can have a lasting effect on the person receiving it.

Overall, positive reinforcement is a pretty simple strategy to employ. Give criticism when needed and recognition when deserved. Keep your team motivated and inspire them to exceed their own expectations. This will obviously benefit them. It will benefit you. And most importantly, it will benefit the organization.

ROLL CALL

Before every shift at the police station, we begin with a roll call. This practice is not just about making sure all officers are accounted for; the supervisor also explains some of the current issues the city is facing. This could involve a series of break-ins, motor vehicle thefts, robberies, or anything else that garners their officers' attention. The supervisor relays any information they currently have surrounding the incidents: dates, times, descriptions of suspects, how they're carrying out the crimes, where they're occurring, and any other related data that would paint a picture of what the officers should be looking for.

This type of communication not only goes on daily, it happens every eight hours for each shift, allowing information to be updated and adjusted based on new facts. To accomplish this kind of information sharing, we rely on a series of communication systems, including portable radios, 911 emergency call centers, and our own police dispatchers. These systems work together seamlessly to provide a real-time information flow that enhances the safety of both the officers and the public. What you should take away from this is to keep information up to date and fluid so that you can continuously adjust your approach without breaking the chain of communication.

Having the most current information when making decisions is advantageous in any setting. Think about it for a second: the law enforcement community utilizes this type of communication to make decisions that could potentially save someone's life. If this is the approach that's relied on for something of that magnitude, its effectiveness must be pretty consistent. You're probably not a police officer and may never want to be one, and that's okay. Even if you work behind a desk in a suit and tie every day, knowing the relevant facts about your business will enable you to allocate your resources accurately, maximizing your results.

Make a conscious effort to have a "roll call" with yourself and with your team on a regular basis, ensuring that everyone is on the same page. This enhances cooperation among team members and decreases the chances of confusion in the workplace. If everyone is hearing the same information, from the same source, at the same time, then there's no excuse for not knowing what's going on. This form of communication counteracts the game of "telephone," where information can be altered, omitted, or misconstrued.

We've all heard the phrase "If you want something done right, do it yourself." I agree with this saying in most cases, but sometimes, especially when undertaking a large endeavor, you have to rely on other people. The good news is that you can still complete a task to your standards without necessarily *doing* it yourself. In order to accomplish that, you need to articulate to the people in charge of overseeing the project what you expect. This is the only way to ensure that all members of your organization have a unified objective.

When I think of a corporate roll call, I view it as a battle plan for the company's future operations. Business is war. It's a world of competition, and business owners are keenly aware of the fact that other companies are always trying to increase their market share. The higher-ups within a company must have a broader perspective of what's going on around them. This is why I believe managers and leaders in all endeavors, from corporations to civic associations, from big companies to mom-and-pop shops, all have an obligation to incorporate a daily or at least a weekly roll call in their plan of operations. The people at the top need to inform everyone of the challenges they're facing and how they plan on countering them. Not only does this keep people up to speed, it gives them a clear understanding of how they can personally assist in combating those challenges with their own performance.

How many times have you walked into a store and encountered an employee with a terrible attitude toward helping you as a consumer? Next time you run into a situation like this, think about everything we just discussed. "But Derrick, maybe they're having a bad day, or they're just a shitty person in general." I can't deny that's a possibility, but it's more likely that this person has been left to do their own thing. The manager of the business has failed to relay what's expected of them. Perhaps that message was conveyed to the employee when they were originally hired, but how many times since? For all you know, the employee has been with the company for ten years and has become complacent over time. You see this a lot with big retail stores that have a massive number of employees. They seem to care more about quantity than quality. How does this happen? It could be for a variety of reasons: low wages, poor work conditions, or a culture where the employee feels disposable. It also may be due to management's failure to reiterate their expectations regarding employee conduct and its relationship to the core values of the company. This lack of communication forces the employees to create their own behavioral standards to follow.

If you had encountered the owner of the business instead, I'm sure you would have had a completely different experience. Owners understand the impact one negative interaction with a customer can have on a company, but it's not enough for them to be aware of it. They also need to make sure that the people they oversee understand that as well. They have to keep the channels of communication open so that everyone at the store shares the same enthusiasm and self-awareness that they have, and this is where having a regular roll call can make a big difference.

The additional advantage of having a roll call is that it's another means of furthering the mission of the company. If your objective is to sell more of a particular product, it's essential that every member of your team understands that goal and believes in the value of achieving it. This group cohesion can only happen if the top people keep in touch with their middle managers. It's then the manager's responsibility to relay that same message to the employees, reminding them periodically of the company's central mission, why it's important, and how to achieve it.

Make it a priority to have a roll call on a regular basis so that you can engrain the organization's mission statement into the people you are leading. And I don't care what you call it: powwows, get-togethers, meetings, briefings, it doesn't matter to me. As long as you're constantly checking in with your team and relaying the most current information available, you'll ensure that the expectations of the organization are understood and put into motion.

Whether you work for a small company or a large corporation, a private business or a government agency, every institution can benefit from the strict adherence to organizational structure and streamlined communication. No one exhibits those two elements more effectively than a paramilitary organization like a police department. Lives depend on their ability to relay information to all employees, from the chief on down to the junior patrolman. The way they accomplish this is by establishing a chain of command and implementing an information-sharing system that functions quickly and accurately.

Although these practices are generally used for law enforcement purposes, many businesses could benefit from the by-products of adopting a similar approach. By applying the same methods used by police officers, you'll create a clearer understanding of organizational values, solve internal conflicts faster, and increase group cohesion.

CHAPTER TEN

||||||||||||||||||||||||||||||||||||||||||||||||||||

LEARN FROM YOUR MISTAKES

No matter how many mistakes you've made in the past, get ready, because you're going to make a few more. Mistakes are inevitable. We all make them, and I'm fairly confident that you've heard someone say that it's important to learn from them. Although that phrase is pretty self-explanatory, I couldn't write a book about improving yourself without addressing this topic, because it's so fundamentally important to personal growth. It's not about how many times you screw up. What's important is what you take away from that experience.

Have you ever been in a position where you've done something you shouldn't have, and the only thing you learned was *not* to do it again? Chances are you have; and that's okay, but it shouldn't be the most significant takeaway. Not repeating a mistake is something that most of us already do, but if that's all that you're getting out of the situation, you're doing yourself a disservice. As much as you may not want to revisit the experience, it's important to dissect what happened and learn as much as you can about yourself and where you went wrong. Review what the situation entailed, how you handled it, and what the outcome was. Think about how you could have handled it differently, resulting in a more desirable outcome.

The majority of the mistakes you make will have very little impact on your life, but anytime you have a setback, you risk limiting your opportunities in the future. I've seen a lot of really good people have a momentary lapse in judgment that instantly alters the course of their life. The decision to get behind the wheel after having too much to drink or getting into a physical altercation that turns deadly are just some of the unfortunate scenarios I've seen play out. These are obviously extreme examples, but they don't have to be this severe to hinder your ability to accomplish your goals. Not devoting yourself to your education, disregarding your personal health, treating your loved ones poorly—these are the types of choices that can limit the options you have moving forward.

I have no problem admitting that I've made a lot of mistakes in my life, and although I'm not proud of some of the things I've done, I wouldn't change them even if I could. The stupid things I did and the consequences I had to deal with as a result of my actions are what molded me into the person I am today. Sometimes people have to learn the hard way, and unfortunately I was one of them. In a weird way, I was one of the lucky ones. I made a lot of poor choices at a very young age, and because of that, I was able to correct them before it was too late. Not everyone is that fortunate. You shouldn't rely on luck in order to adapt. It's our responsibility to analyze what we did wrong and identify our downfalls. Don't be the person who says, "Man, I won't do *that* again" and moves on with their life as if nothing happened. What you *should* be doing is asking yourself:

Why, What, and How:
- "Why did I do it?"
- "What did I do wrong?"
- "How should I have handled it differently?"

These are the questions that will keep you from committing the same offense down the road.

No one's perfect. No matter how hard you try to do everything right, sometimes things will go wrong. Do whatever you can to limit those occurrences, but when they do happen, don't run from them. Break them down into their most simplistic form and figure out how to use what you've learned to your advantage in the future.

YOUR CHOICES TODAY WILL AFFECT
YOUR OPPORTUNITIES TOMORROW

I grew up in a family of four children. Both of my parents worked hard and did the best they could, but we never had a ton of money. Like a lot of families out there, we lived paycheck to paycheck. Because of this, I didn't always have the nicest things. Kids at school had newer clothes, bigger homes, and were dropped off in nicer cars. It was easy to become bitter and jealous, and many times I fell into the trap of feeling that way. I felt that it wasn't fair. That feeling led me to act out and rebel against my teachers and family as an eleven-year-old. I was getting into fights, hanging out with the wrong people, skipping school, and even when I did attend, I wasn't applying myself. Most of the time I slept through class until the teacher caught me. This went on for nearly a year, and it almost resulted in my not graduating from the fifth grade. I was making a lot of mistakes. But luckily for me, something happened that turned the entire situation around. I met someone totally unexpected, someone whom I wouldn't have met if it weren't for the mistakes I was making.

We had a social worker at our school by the name of Matt. He mostly dealt with troubled kids who were having issues at home and not participating in class. His job was to talk with these students and try to put them on the right path. When Matt and I first met, I wasn't really open to the idea of talking with him about what was going on at home. I thought he was going to be just like the teachers I had spoken with before him, explaining how "things could be worse." I thought he really didn't care about what was going on in my life and was just doing his job. But I was wrong. He was different. He didn't force me to speak. He didn't constantly ask me what was wrong or whether I wanted to talk about it. Instead, we had conversations about sports, girls, video games, school—you name it. Eventually, I opened up to him about how I was feeling, and he listened while I vented. He didn't judge me or try to make excuses for what I was going through. Instead, he told me something that would stick with me for the rest of my life.

He looked at me and said, "Derrick, I'm going to say something that you might not like. You haven't been dealt the best hand."

Finally! Someone had actually acknowledged that everything wasn't perfect and that I wasn't just making it up. I was shocked. Everyone else had always tried to spin it, and here he was shooting me straight. *Now* he had my attention. He continued:

"You don't have everything. I get it. There are definitively some kids that have more than you, but I'm going to tell you some good news. You get to decide the second half of your future. You get to choose who your family is, who your friends are, what you do for work, and how much money you make. But there's a caveat to that… It starts now. You have to start doing well in school, you have to hang out with the right friends, and you have to really want it. Because what you do today will affect the opportunities you have tomorrow."

There it was…exactly what I had needed even though I didn't know it at the time. *Hope*. Matt had given me a way out. Although things weren't great now, if I did what he said, if I stopped making the same mistakes, I would decide my future. I would determine how much money I made, what clothes I wore, what my kids would have, and what cars I'd drive. And I really wanted to have those options.

So I started applying myself. I stopped hanging around with the wrong people, and I got involved in sports, motivated by the thought that if I stayed on course, I would eventually have all the things I wanted. Fortunately, I was able to turn it around in time and was assigned to the sixth grade. Being "assigned" meant that I didn't pass the fifth grade, but as long as I showed improvement during the first quarter of the sixth grade, I would be allowed to stay…and luckily for me, I did.

When I was in the *Big Brother* house, I had a lot of time to reflect. There's no contact with the outside world for three months, so essentially your life is on pause for that time. I remember sitting outside on the couch for hours, just looking up at the sky, thinking about the fifth grade and how the choices I made after meeting Matt had led me to that point. I also thought about the mistakes I made, and the fact that if I hadn't learned from them, I wouldn't have had this opportunity. A lot of the kids I had been hanging out with were either dead or in jail. That easily could have been me. I was one of the lucky ones.

Matt was right all along. By choosing not to repeatedly make the same mistakes over and over, I did choose my own future. I have a beautiful family, earned two college degrees, won half a million dollars on my favorite TV show, and have had some amazing opportunities that I never thought would be possible. All because of the decision I made when I was eleven years old.

The purpose of this story is not to make you feel all warm and fuzzy inside. But if it does, that's fine, because it sure as hell makes *me* feel that way when I look back on it. I'm extremely proud of what I've done with the hand I was dealt. My intention is to show you that regardless of your age or where you are in life, the mistakes you make can have a profound impact on your future. Whether that impact is positive or negative is ultimately up to you.

LIVING PROOF

I'm not perfect. I've never claimed to be. In fact, I could write a book on all the mistakes I've made in my life. Yes, I got my act together after realizing the possible ramifications of my behavior, but that doesn't mean that I was an angel from that point forward.

When I think about my life and some of the mistakes I've

made, the first person that crosses my mind is my poor mom. I put that woman through hell, but I have to give her credit—she was always there for me.

I'm sitting here trying to think of some good examples to share with you, and the sad thing is that there were so many, I'm probably forgetting a few. My mom and I joke about it now, but only because I was able to straighten myself out. I can promise you that she wasn't laughing when they were actually happening. Skipping school and getting into fights weren't even my biggest issues. Where I *really* crossed the line was when I did things like drink alcohol in the school bathroom. That one didn't go over too well at school *or* at home.

Another incident happened while I was playing baseball in college. Each year, we would travel to Florida for spring training. The trip started out great, but unfortunately, it didn't end that way. The first three days that we were there, the team morale was high and we were playing well. We hadn't lost a game up to that point. On the fourth day, the coaches decided to have a quick practice before our next game. They left it up to us to choose whether we wanted to wear shorts or baseball pants; whatever the majority decision was, we all had to wear the same thing.

It was a hot day, so most of the team wanted to wear shorts. Our starting shortstop, who was a transfer student from another school, had a different mind-set. He thought that we should   all wear pants, and he made his opinion known. As one of the leaders on the team, I pulled him aside and told him that we had made a group decision and he needed to let it go. He kept to himself the whole time at practice, and his reclusive behavior carried over to the game the following day.

It was a night game and there were a lot of fans in the bleachers. We were in the outfield, warming up as a team as we did before every game. I was leading the stretches with my best friend, Nick, but the shortstop had decided to stay in the dugout. Now to be fair, stretching with the team wasn't mandatory, but it was a pregame ritual, and no one had ever sat in the dugout before. He was trying to make a point, and for some reason it really got to me. I took it personally. When the team finished stretching, he came out to play catch with Nick and I cut him off in his tracks. I got right in his face, pointed my finger two inches from his nose, and told him that if he ever did that again, we were going to have a "misunderstanding." And what I actually meant by that, well… I'll leave that for you to interpret on you own.

The entire incident took place in front of the team, the coaches, and the fans. And I wasn't quiet about it; they could clearly hear everything I had to say, profanities and all. Nick eventually pulled the shortstop away to defuse the situation and the game went on.

We lost.

And we didn't just lose, we got *crushed*. What made it even worse was that we had already beaten this team earlier in the week. The unexpected loss really affected our team chemistry, and we ended up losing all of our remaining games. I distinctly remember it being a very quiet flight back home to Connecticut. So, did we lose the rest of our games because of what had happened? Maybe. We'll never know for sure, but I think it's safe to assume that it definitely didn't help.

When we got home and the coaches had time to talk about what had occurred, they decided to suspend me for two games. I was heartbroken. I loved the guys on my team and wasn't even given the opportunity to tell my side of the story. I didn't feel that I had done anything wrong, and contemplated quitting the team altogether, even though I was on a scholarship. My suspension ended after only one game because numerous players spoke to the coaching staff on my behalf.

Although they reduced my suspension, it didn't change the fact that I *was* wrong. I handled the situation poorly and my approach should have been completely different. I should have set a better example for my team by choosing a more appropriate time to voice my concerns. Not only did my behavior result in a suspension, it could have been a lot worse. I almost quit the team out of principle, a move that would have cost my parents a lot of money and made me miss out on some of my best memories in sports. I decided right then and there that I wouldn't make the same mistake twice. I saw the error of my ways and changed how I conducted myself as a leader.

By reflecting on past mistakes, you can improve future outcomes. Don't just view them as a setback, treat them as a learning experience, serving as a constant reminder of what *not* to do.

CRITIQUE YOUR CHARACTER FLAWS

We talked about knowing your weaknesses in the first chapter, but that discussion was more about identifying areas of your skill set that need improvement. In the same way, you can break down your social miscues by analyzing how they occurred and the way you handled them to identify character flaws. Are you a jealous person? Are you defensive when receiving criticism? Are you impatient? These are just a few of the personality traits you can identify by reviewing your past conduct.

One of my first jobs was working at a local store in the furniture department. There were a few other employees, and we all had different responsibilities, but our main priority was selling furniture. I remember one salesman who used to unintentionally intimidate people with how aggressive he was. He would ask them if they needed anything and then hover over them while they continued to look around. It was uncomfortable to watch, so I could only imagine how it felt for the people shopping. Most of the time, the customers would end up leaving without buying anything. I felt bad for the guy because he was actually a really nice person. Unfortunately, he had no clue that his behavior was actually pushing people away.

One day, while we were on a break, he was venting about his lack of sales. He was talking to me but he was also kind of talking to himself. I could tell that his wheels were turning. At one point during his complaining he stopped and said, "From now on, I'm going to introduce myself, ask if they have any questions, and then walk away. If they need me, they'll find me."

Before he could say another word, I immediately replied, "Yeah. You should give that a shot." In my head I was actually saying, "Thank god! He's finally on to something."

Over the next couple of months, he followed through on what he said he was going to do, and it worked. In fact, customers were approaching me and asking where he was because they couldn't find him! Eventually he found a happy medium, and he began to make sales more consistently.

I didn't get to know him that well, but I can only assume that he was probably overly aggressive in numerous aspects of his life. But by taking the time to break down his behavior in this particular situation, he was able to identify his flaws and correct them. Using his experience in the furniture department as a reference, hopefully he was able to also make improvements in his personal life by incorporating a similar philosophy.

The takeaway from this story is that not only can you improve your *current* situation by identifying your downfalls, you can also apply that same knowledge to *future* scenarios. That's how you make the trials and tribulations you experience today benefit you tomorrow—by going into a situation one way and coming out with a deeper understanding of who you are and how to overcome your shortcomings.

It's not always easy for us to identify our own flaws, and that's where our friends come into play. Usually, you can find one or two close friends who are more than willing to give you a reality check. It's not that uncommon for friends to casually drop subtle hints about things you're doing to your own detriment. For me, I sometimes say what I'm thinking when I really shouldn't. I have definitely had friends mention that I needed to be more careful, because I've pissed some people off with my words. The scary thing is that if they hadn't said anything to me, I would've never known. Because of their input, I'm more cognizant of what I say around other people now. So don't be offended if you get put in your place once in a while. They're probably doing it for your own good. Embrace the criticism and learn from it.

It's great to have honest friends, but what happens when you don't have anyone who's willing to call you out? For some people, talking with a professional can provide objective feedback on their deficiencies. The notion that seeking help from a therapist or doctor is a sign of weakness is simply not true. In some cases, it may be the only way to open your awareness to some things about yourself that you otherwise wouldn't notice.

I have a friend who sees a therapist on a regular basis. He doesn't get into the details about why he goes, but I know he had some issues growing up as a kid. He had a really tough childhood with an abusive father, and I know he still thinks about it sometimes. On the exterior, he strikes me as perfectly normal, so I've asked him why he feels the need to speak with a complete stranger.

"It's helpful to hear another person's view on the decisions I'm making," he said. He uses his therapist the way you might talk with a friend, bouncing ideas off of them to get a different opinion. "When I wanted to buy a new car, I was all set on getting it, but it was very expensive," he said. "My therapist didn't tell me flat out not to buy it, but they brought up the fact that I had bought a new Mustang right out of college and ruined my credit when I couldn't pay for it. It was something that I had already thought about but just ignored. When you have someone who has no skin in the game tell you that it's a bad idea, you tend to listen." If you're struggling to pinpoint the areas in your life that need improvement or you're unsure of how to handle a dilemma you're currently facing, don't be afraid to see someone. More people than you think choose to take this route. And if you don't think you know anyone who has ever talked to a professional before, you're wrong, because *I* have. So there's at least one person you now know.

Your social missteps are a wake-up call, but only if you recognize them. It pays to do some self-analysis, consult with friends, or speak with a professional when seeking objective feedback on what you're doing wrong. Identifying the flaws in your personality and their effect on your conduct is a key component to personal development. Those who understand that our behavior is just as vital to our success as our actual abilities will embrace this process and grow from it.

DON'T BE A HYPOCRITE

We've talked a lot about learning from your mistakes and identifying your character flaws, which can affect your personal growth. Well, that doesn't only apply to you. It's important to remember that the people in your life—your family, your friends, colleagues, employers, employees—they're all growing too. So when you witness their mistakes, whether they directly affect you or not, have compassion. Understand that in order to become better versions of themselves, they're going to screw up once in a while.

It's not only about *their* mistake; it's also how *you* react to the situation that determines what they learn from it. If a child has a momentary lapse in judgment, they should understand that what they did was wrong, but they shouldn't be afraid of it happening again. Don't create an environment where they're fearful of your reaction and decide not to tell you at all. How can you help them if they won't talk to you? Create a culture that accepts mistakes and recognizes them as a necessary part of learning.

And this isn't only for your children; this applies to employees or anyone else who feels an obligation to inform you of a poor decision. I have a friend who is a manager at a local bank and she's responsible for all of the tellers. At the end of every shift, the tellers must count the money remaining in their cash drawers, and if done correctly, the money should match their register receipts. A few months ago, there was one teller whose drawer was off by a couple of dollars almost every day. Not only was it an inconvenience to go back and figure out why the money didn't match up, the manager wasn't allowed to leave until the issue was rectified. The teller's problem turned into management's problem, and my friend's frustration was visible to everyone at the bank. Her negative reaction to the teller's miscalculations led to the teller taking money out or adding her own money in to balance the drawer. This was obviously not an appropriate solution and my friend had to fire her.

I respect my friend and what she does, but I think this was a situation that could have been handled differently. It sounds to me like the teller was so afraid to inform the manager of her mistake that she tried to correct it on her own, causing an even bigger issue. What if my friend had been more approachable? What if she had been more understanding about the situation and offered a solution to the problem, rather than creating fear?

Unfortunately, we'll never know for sure, but remember this example. If you're in a managerial role, create a culture where people know that mistakes are frowned upon but acceptable under certain circumstances. We want the individuals we're responsible for to feel comfortable explaining their errors, knowing that we won't be happy about it, but that we'll still contribute to the conversation in a positive manner. Don't concentrate on what they did wrong. Turn the situation into an opportunity to show them how to do it right.

WHEN GOOD INTENTIONS GO WRONG

Life is a constant education. Some things can't be taught, they have to be experienced. With everything we do, there's a lesson to be learned. And sometimes those lessons come when least expected. I wrote this book with the hope of possibly helping the reader. The irony is that it actually helped me. I didn't expect it, but by writing my thoughts down on paper, I put more emphasis on following my own advice.

Over the last year, I've had a lot going on in my life. In addition to working at the police department, I had a new baby, a new television show, and this book. While evaluating my own life choices, I concluded that I was making a glaring mistake: I was so caught up in pursuing my personal ambitions that I wasn't spending enough time with my kids. The excuse I always made for myself was that everything I was doing would provide a better life for them in the future. But what about now? What about the memories I was missing out on *today*?

When I was traveling, my wife would send me photos and videos of the different things they were doing together: hanging out at family cookouts, going apple picking, and playing in the park. I was seeing these things, but I wasn't living them. When my daughters reminisced about these moments, they would also remember that I wasn't there. The thought of them making that association did not sit well with me. I had good intentions, but nevertheless I was wrong. I needed to make changes immediately, and that started with viewing my family as a priority rather than obligation.

In an attempt to make up for lost time, I told my wife that regardless of what was going on, we were going on a family vacation, and that I really wanted to take the girls to Disney World. We started looking into flights, and I booked the tickets before we even had passes to the parks. I wanted to commit to going before I made excuses why we shouldn't.

We ended up flying down to Florida in October, and it was even better than expected. It wasn't what we did or who we saw that made it so special; it was the little things. I remember sitting on the plane with Tenley and Peyton while we watched a movie together. Just sitting there, holding both of them in my arms—that was what I had been missing out on. No accomplishment in my career would ever be more fulfilling than what I felt at that very moment.

The reason I'm sharing these stories is not to make this discussion about me or to turn this book into my personal journal. It's an acknowledgment that no matter what we do or how hard we try to make the right choices, we're going to make mistakes. We have to recognize that self-improvement is a constant evolution and that, although we may think we have a good handle on life, we're still learning as we go.

While I was writing this very chapter, the presidential race between Hillary Clinton and Donald Trump came to a conclusion. With the media so focused on these two individuals, it gave me some insight as to how politicians approach their mistakes, which I think we can all learn from. Some of them don't own up to anything. They dig their heels in and deny, deny, deny. Unless you literally show them physical proof of what they did wrong, they'll never admit to it, and even when you have proof, they'll find a way to spin it. On the other hand, the smart politicians quickly apologize when they have a lapse in judgment. They take responsibility for their mistakes in an attempt to learn from what they've done. The public usually accepts their apology and is quick to forgive and forget. There is definitely a lesson to be learned here for all of us.

Owning up to our mistakes is not necessarily a bad thing. It's the first step on the road to personal improvement. One of the hardest things for some people to do is to admit when they're wrong. None of us want to be seen as a failure, but when you get right down to it, failing is a part of living. *That's* what makes us human.

Our lives are molded by the choices we make. Whether it's a personal choice pertaining to the way you conduct yourself or a decision that requires a simple "yes" or "no," it's all relevant to defining who you are as a person. Where you want to be in life is ultimately up to you. Whether you actually get there will hinge not only on your ability to make the right decisions, but also on how you handle yourself when you make the wrong ones.

CHAPTER ELEVEN

||||||||||||||||||||||||||||||||||||||||||||||||||||||

GROW THROUGH ADVERSITY

Life is bound to throw you a curveball once in a while. But it's not always just a curveball—sometimes it's a grenade. The interesting thing about adversities is that they're not always a product of your behavior. Sometimes things go wrong even when you're doing everything right.

Adversity can become one of two things: it can be a *stepping-stone* on your path to personal growth or an *obstacle* that you can't overcome. What it ultimately represents is up to you. And I'm not saying that the choices you'll have to make when facing adversity will be easy. Dealing with misfortune is not as simple as saying, "I want to learn from this experience." You have to find peace with what occurred and develop a means of understanding why it happened to you.

One of my mother's favorite sayings is, "God won't give you more than you can handle." That may be true, but being *capable* of handling something doesn't mean you should have to. Overall, I think that I've been pretty fortunate. Yes, I've been through my ups and downs, but in comparison to some of the stories I hear, I've been lucky. That doesn't mean that there haven't been obstacles in my life that I've had to overcome. Hell, I found out on national television that my grandfather had passed away while I was trapped on a studio lot. I assume I'm one of the only people in the world who can say that.

There have been points in my life when I didn't know how it was going to work out. I've been at rock bottom, and I know what it feels like to lose hope. If you're dealing with difficulties in your life and feel like there's no way out, I'm here to tell you that you're wrong. I've experienced rough times at work and in my personal life, where the majority of the people didn't think I'd recover. They had already written me off. Most of them assumed that it was too much to overcome, and there were moments when I thought that they were right. Even with my own self-doubt, I knew it was up to me to prove them wrong. I decided that I was going to use my negative experiences as *motivation* rather than as an *excuse*. That decision allowed me to correct my own course.

When you look objectively at life, there are always more

punches being received than being thrown. This impartial assessment also reveals an important but disheartening fact: we're all destined to experience profound adversity at some point in our lives. No matter how hard we try to avoid it, the unexpected is always one second away. How many times have you heard a sad story start with "Everything was fine, and then all of a sudden…"? Some of the most devastating blows can come when you least expect them. It's life's way of throwing a sucker punch, and how we react under those adverse conditions is more important than the dilemma itself. At some point, we all deal with hardship, but your ability to grow from those experiences is what separates your successes from your failures.

Through my struggles, I've learned to take a different approach to dealing with life's unexpected roadblocks. I now see adversity as a springboard to personal development. It's a rare opportunity to advance your understanding of what you're capable of handling. The only way to really know if you'll refuse to quit when the odds are stacked against you is by putting yourself to the test. I refuse to believe that some things are just too problematic to overcome. Use whatever difficulty you face as a chance to grow. Turn adversity into opportunity.

LIFE OR DEATH

It happened on April 8, 2007. A man called the emergency line, stated that he needed help, and then hung up the phone. The call was traced back to 71 Rand Street, second-floor apartment. I wasn't actually dispatched to the call, but I was training a new officer and figured it was a chance to give the rookie some experience. Rand Street was a short drive from the police station, and we were the first ones to arrive. After two other officers showed up, we all walked toward the entrance of the building. 911 emergency calls were a common occurrence, and most of them turned out to be false alarms. So as we made our way to the door, we were all pretty relaxed and actually discussed how slow of a night it had been. That was about to change.

Before going any further, you have to understand the layout of the Rand Street address. Most homes in Central Falls are what we call "triple-deckers." They're one building with three separate apartments on top of one another, and they all share a common stairwell. These homes are mostly found in urban areas, so if you live in the city, you're probably familiar with this type of residential housing.

As we entered the building, we went right up to the second floor. When we got there, a couple of individuals who spoke very little English directed us to the third floor. The two other officers with me spoke Spanish, and they gathered from the witnesses that there had been some type of altercation prior to our arrival.

The stairway was very narrow, so as we made our way up to the third floor, we had to walk in a single file. I was first in line, and as I turned the corner, I saw a middle-aged man at the top of the stairs, just staring down at me. It looked a little creepy, but I'd be lying if I said I hadn't encountered things like that before, so it didn't really raise my suspicion.

I said "Hello," but he didn't answer. As I walked up a few more steps, I noticed a broken knife on one of the stairs and pointed it out to the officers behind me. When we reached the unidentified male, I stepped onto the third-floor landing and stood to his right, allowing the other officer to speak with him in Spanish. From my angle, I could see almost everything, including the entrance to the third-floor apartment. The only thing standing between me and the door was this middle-aged man.

While the officer spoke with the man in Spanish, I watched their faces, trying to get a sense of what they were discussing. From the guy's tone of voice, it sounded like the fight was already over. I was just waiting for the word from my colleague that they no longer needed our assistance. But then, unexpectedly, the man reached over and opened the apartment door. It swung completely open, and I had a direct view into the apartment.

The other officers were still on the stairs and couldn't see what I was seeing. The entire apartment was in darkness except for one room near the far left corner. I couldn't see into the room itself, but I had a clear view of the doorway, which was illuminated. I didn't know why the man had opened the door or what he was trying to show me, but now he had my full attention.

The apartment door was only open for a few seconds before a figure peeked out from the illuminated room. In the shadows, all I could make out was a head. I could tell that the individual was looking at me, but whoever it was, they didn't say a word. My gut was telling me that something wasn't right about this person. Why did they look out from the room so slowly? What exactly were they doing before we got there?

Then all at once the person stepped out a little further, and I could see a silhouette of their entire body. I could tell that it was a man and that his arms were down by his side. He turned toward me and began to approach the apartment door. For a brief second, I got a glimpse of an object he was holding, and I immediately knew what it was.

"Knife!" I yelled.

I pushed the man in front of me down the stairs so I could draw my firearm. The other officers didn't know what the hell was going on or why I had just thrown this guy in their direction.

The assailant with the knife rushed the apartment door but stopped abruptly in the entranceway. I tried to back up as much as I could to create some space between us, but my right shoulder hit something, forcing me to stop. Then I felt a breeze on my back. I was up against the frame of a large open window. One inch further and I would have fallen three stories to the pavement below.

The knife-wielding man stared right into my eyes as he raised the weapon to his chest and pointed it in my direction. He was angry, and it appeared that he was under the influence of alcohol or drugs, but all I could do at that point was keep my firearm aimed at his chest. I repeatedly instructed him to drop the knife, but he refused. The blood was pounding in my ears, and I knew we were at a make-or-break point.

Moving without warning, he quickly retreated into the apartment, slamming the entrance door and locking himself inside.

I looked at the other officers. Their eyes were glued to mine, waiting for direction. I knew we had to go in after him. We didn't know if there was anyone else in the apartment whom he intended to hurt, or if he was planning on harming himself. There was no time to waste. I took a deep breath, knowing what was waiting for me on the other side of that door, and then kicked it open with everything I had.

The kitchen was dark as we entered, but one of the officers had his flashlight on, allowing me to clearly see the suspect standing in the back corner of the room, still holding the knife. He faced us in a fighting stance as he raised the knife above his head. He kept lunging forward as if he was going to attack us, but he never did. Although we were all yelling at him to drop the knife, in both English and in Spanish, you could tell that he had no intention of doing so. That was when I knew that it was going to end badly.

When the man realized that we weren't leaving, he ran

down a small hallway that led to the living room. We immediately followed, but because of the narrowness of the hallway, we had to stack into a single line, and I was at the front. I advanced to the doorway of the living room and stopped before entering so I could see where he was. The room was small, maybe ten feet by ten feet. There was a window on the back wall that led to a fire escape, which he intended to use to avoid being apprehended. When he saw me standing in the room, still pleading with him to drop the knife, he decided that there were only two ways this was going to end. He was going to kill me or I was going to kill him.

It only took a second for him to make his move. He raised the knife over his head and ran straight toward me. I gave it one last attempt and demanded that he drop the knife, but he had already made up his mind. I aimed my firearm at his chest and pulled the trigger. I heard two loud bangs and saw his shirt tear open, but he didn't even break his stride. I fired two additional shots in an attempt to stop him, and although he continued forward, he was severely injured and no longer a threat. He crashed into the wall to the right of me and then crumpled to the floor. Even though he was badly hurt, he was still holding the knife. I had to actually kick it out of his hand in order to remove it.

We immediately called for emergency personnel to respond and tend to his injuries, but when I looked in his eyes I knew he wasn't going to make it. I was only twenty-three years old, and there I was, standing over a man whom I had just shot.

As I looked around, the room was filled with smoke and I had a sharp ringing in my right ear, but I didn't know why. It wasn't until later that I learned that the officer standing behind me had also shot the suspect twice while his gun was next to my ear.

Moments later, rescue workers arrived and attempted to resuscitate the man. I stepped outside so that they could do their job. I sat on a wall in the driveway to collect my thoughts and steady my nerves. As I was sitting there trying to wrap my head around what had just happened, the emergency personnel exited the building and slowly walked back to the ambulance. I looked at one of them and asked, "Did he make it?"

He glanced at me and replied, "No. Sorry." He had confirmed what I had already known. I had just taken a man's life. In a matter of seconds, on a call that I wasn't even originally dispatched to, my life was changed forever.

THE AFTERMATH

That night was the most traumatic event I've ever experienced, but the months that followed were equally stressful. Everyone told me that I had done the right thing, but there was still a procedure I had to go through before I could return to work. Every police-involved shooting is investigated by the state police and then presented to a grand jury, which decides whether or not to indict the officer. This is a lengthy process. It can often take months, and in the meantime the court of public opinion is already in session. Few details are released about the shooting, since it's an ongoing investigation, but that doesn't stop anyone from forming their own conclusions.

"They shot him while he was cutting carrots."

"The cops didn't speak Spanish, so the man didn't understand what they were saying."

These were only a couple of the false allegations I heard while waiting for my day in court. All I could do was sit at home on administrative leave and go to my mandatory counseling (I told you I had seen a therapist), which at first I was totally against. I remember waking up some mornings and actually feeling a little better about the situation. I would take a shower, get dressed, and cook breakfast. I'd make plans to work out and maybe clean my truck. I was motivated and ready to get the day underway. But then I would make the mistake of reading the newspaper, and my day would go to shit. This became a common chain of events following the incident, but eventually I learned not to read the papers or watch the news.

It wasn't long before my case was heard by the grand jury. This was where the decision would be made as to whether or not the actions of myself and the other officers were justified. The days leading up to my testimony were some of the most stressful times of the entire experience. I would lie in bed and think to myself that a group of twenty people who had been watching the news and had no idea who I was would be deciding my fate. Honestly, I thought I was screwed.

When it came time to testify, the jury asked some tough questions but for the most part, they were reasonable. There were a couple of questions like "Why didn't you tackle him instead of shooting him?" or "Why didn't you use pepper spray on him first?" I knew that these people had my freedom in their hands, so I gave my reasons, and I could tell by their body language that my answers were acceptable.

After hearing testimony from everyone involved with the incident, the grand jury came back with a decision after deliberating for only one day. Based on all the facts surrounding the case, it was ruled that our actions were appropriate and that we should not be indicted. I remember picking up the phone and hearing my lieutenant on the other end say, "They came back no true bill. You did a great job, Derrick." I cannot describe the relief I felt at that moment. I hung up the phone and sat in silence for almost an hour. The nightmare was finally over...or at least I thought it was.

Even though I had been cleared of any wrongdoing, something didn't feel right. I might not have made it to church every

Sunday, but I grew up being exposed to religious ideas, and I believed in most of them. I started to think about the afterlife, and I began to wonder if my actions violated the beliefs I had grown up practicing.

I became reckless. I bought a motorcycle and found myself doing stupid things like riding in the rain at high speeds. I was drinking alcohol more often and waking up in random places, like my mother's porch. I was more irritable and easily agitated by insignificant matters. While I was going through this tough time, the police department informed me that I was being recommended for a Medal of Valor. This is the highest award an officer can receive, and I didn't even care. Honestly, I didn't even know if I wanted to be a cop anymore.

I tried to find things to do that would distract me, but when I was alone in my room with the lights off, the ringing in my ear would become louder, and all I could think about was the shooting. I'd replay the whole incident in my head over and over. I even started to second-guess myself. Was there something I could have done differently? Had I really done everything I could?

One night, I went out, because I had been fighting with the majority of my family members and desperately needed to clear my head. I drank all evening and had to be driven home by a friend. I was so drunk that he couldn't even carry me into my house, so he left me on the back porch to sleep it off. When I finally woke up,

I crawled to my room and into my bed. The room was in complete darkness. All I could do was stare at the ceiling. My vision was blurry, and I could smell booze on my breath. I could see the path I was on and knew I had to make a change or my behavior would eventually kill me. I sat up, put my face in my hands, and started crying. Then I got angry. Not at the situation, but at myself. This wasn't *me*. I thought about Matt, the social worker who had helped me as a young man, who had taught me that the future was mine to make. I could hear his voice saying, "You didn't go through everything you went through and work as hard as you did to throw it all away."

No matter how much I might have wanted to alter the past, that wasn't an option. Nothing on earth was going to change what had happened. I knew I had to make a choice. I could let this nightmare consume me...or I could take what I had experienced and grow from it. The direction I went was entirely up to me.

I decided not to let what I had been through define me. It was time to move on. I started by devoting myself to my counseling. Richard, my counselor, would give me books to read, and instead of throwing them in the back seat of my car, I would actually read them. I also met with the police chaplain, who assured me that God would not view my actions as a sin because my intentions were pure, and that was something I really needed to hear. I stayed away from the partying and the booze and got myself back into the gym. I was determined to take this awful experience and turn it into the most important life lesson I would ever learn.

The entire experience taught me that life is precious, and it can be taken from you in a matter of seconds. We only get one opportunity to live on this earth, so why waste it? It's important to make the most out of every opportunity, because you may not get a second chance at it.

When I initially became a police officer, one of my main goals was to one day be promoted to detective. After eight months of not only getting back to who I was before the shooting, but becoming a better version of myself, I returned to work. A few months later, I was promoted to the rank of detective. Some of the best memories I have of my career were during my time as an investigator. I had watched a ton of movies about undercover detectives tracking down the bad guys and finding the drugs, and now I was doing it for a living. I learned a lot about myself during that time—and got to see firsthand what my life could have been like if I hadn't made the right decisions growing up.

Working undercover forced me to get close with a lot of bad people. If I wanted to gain their trust, I had to build a personal relationship with them. When they needed someone to confide in, I was always willing to lend an ear. Sitting down and talking about our pasts made me realize something: we weren't all that different. Although our current situations were worlds apart, they were both

the result of the choices we made. It really wasn't that complicated—they had chosen one path, and I had chosen the other.

The experiences I gained, and the life lessons I learned while
working as a detective—I would have missed out on *all* of them if
I had let the adversities following my shooting defeat me.

That day altered my outlook on life. I changed the way I
approached everything. I made a promise to myself to never avoid
doing something because it was too difficult or too time consum-
ing. I wouldn't push it off to a later date, because none of us are
guaranteed tomorrow. If I wanted something, I was going for it.

I wanted to go back to school and further my education, so I
enrolled in night school. I wanted to buy my first home and start
a family, so I bought a house and moved in with Jana, who is
now my wife. Then I got this crazy idea to go on my favorite TV
show—and you know how that one turned out. I wanted to write
a book about my experiences, including my shooting, with the
hope of it having a positive effect on someone else's life. The only
person who can tell me if I succeeded with that one is *you*.

I often think about that pivotal night in my room when I
decided not to let my current situation define me. I reflect back
on everything I've been able to accomplish since making that
life-changing decision. I won't lie to you: I still think about the
shooting all the time. But instead of viewing it as something I want
to forget, I see it as a moment I need to remember. The whole

ordeal serves as a constant reminder to never let fear hold me back from pursuing my goals. It gives me the confidence to tackle any task, regardless of what the doubters say. It reassures me that in the face of adversity, I can overcome anything.

When you experience misfortune, don't run from it. See it for what it is, and confront the problem with the mind-set that regardless of what you're going through, *you* control your future. Take a step back, evaluate your current situation, and find a way to prevail.

VERSION 2.0

I mentioned earlier in the book that I love technology. I'm the guy who's always checking to make sure that I have the latest software installed on all my devices. Consider the adversity you went through, and the knowledge you gained from it, your own personal software upgrade. Your new outlook on life is now version 2.0.

My shooting was obviously a very difficult time in my life, and I hope you never have to go through anything that traumatic. But the reality is, unfortunately, you might. It may not involve something as severe as a shooting, but it doesn't have to rise to that magnitude in order to qualify as an extremely challenging event. It could be the death of a family member, losing your job, or an unexpected injury or illness.

Look at all the people who are perfectly fine one day, and then the next day find out that they have cancer or some other life-threatening condition. Their entire existence is completely flipped upside-down in a matter of minutes. Some people will fight hard but still lose their battle. Others are fortunate enough to survive and, in most cases, come out of it with a different level of clarity about life. They realize the importance of pursing their goals today, rather than holding them off until tomorrow. And when they make a decision to do something, they no longer seek the approval of the people who don't matter to them.

After returning home from *Big Brother*, I learned that a few of my colleagues weren't very supportive of my decision to go on the show. They bitched and complained the entire time I was gone. My decision didn't affect them in the least, but that didn't matter. It wasn't normal (in their opinion) for a cop to appear on a reality show. Before I left for Los Angeles, certain individuals made complaints, talked behind my back, and tried to deter me from going. There was even a last-ditch effort to stop me from leaving when an "anonymous caller" contacted city hall a week before I left. The person claimed that they knew I was going on a show and that my absence would have a negative impact on the police department.

Here's what you may find surprising about the whole situation: I *knew* that people would react this way. I knew that certain individuals would be upset about me going. In fact, I would've been surprised if they hadn't reacted the way they did. But truthfully, I didn't care. I wasn't doing it for them; I was doing it for me and my family. I wasn't going to base my decision on the opinions of people who didn't matter to me. This was a once-in-a-lifetime opportunity, and I wasn't going to make the mistake of letting it pass me by.

Before my experience with the shooting and the events that followed, I probably would have felt differently about leaving the police department to pursue a personal goal. There's a very strong possibility that I would have played it safe and chosen not to leave. I would have allowed outside influences to ultimately make my decision for me. But because of what I had been through, I was a stronger version of myself. I knew better than to let someone else control my fate. I was "Derrick 2.0."

There will be times in your life when you're faced with a scenario that could be a whole lot easier if you would just conform or take the easy route. Refrain from doing that. Adversity doesn't have to be a negative thing. One of the most gratifying feelings you can experience happens when you beat the odds. Pick and choose your battles, but when confronted with an obstacle that seems like a complete loss, think before running away from it. Yes, there are some things you can't change, but that doesn't mean you still can't benefit from the experience. Treat the adversities you face as a personal challenge. Learn to put problems into perspective, filing them in your mind as life lessons that have the potential to help you later. Don't resign yourself to accepting your current circumstances when there are things within your power that can improve your position in life.

Are you the type of person who's going to let adversity dictate your future, or are you someone who will succeed in spite of the hardships you endure? Only *you* can answer that question.

||||||||||||||||||||||||||||||||||||||||||||||||||||||||||||||||

CHAPTER TWELVE

SURROUND YOURSELF
WITH INSPIRATION

Regardless of how talented or successful a person may be, every-one has someone they look up to. And for most of us, there is the typical progression that we all go through. As kids, we look to our parents for guidance. As teenagers, we observe the actions of our teachers and coaches. But as we transition into adulthood, choos-ing who we model ourselves after becomes more complex.

Your first instinct may be to look to a supervisor or an employer to be a mentor. But it doesn't have to be someone in a managerial role; it could also be a colleague. Then again, your role model might be a family member or a friend. Or it could be someone that you don't even personally know, like an author, a celebrity, or someone who's been successful in the business world.

The truth is, it really doesn't matter *who* you look to for inspiration. What does matter is what they represent and the aspect of their life you're hoping to emulate. Call them a role model, an idol, a mentor—that's up to you. Whatever name you choose, it all means the same thing: these are the people you admire. And because you respect them, it's likely that they'll have an influence on how you conduct yourself and the decisions you make.

Understand that you may not find everything you need in one mentor. If you're like most people, you'll have multiple role models. Depending on what you're looking to achieve, you might have twenty of them, and all for slightly different reasons. You might respect someone because of their creativity and willingness to constantly push the envelope in the name of innovation. Then there might be another person with a proven track record in business who influences your own work ethic and management style. Or it could be someone you admire because of their personal wealth and physical possessions. If it's not about knowledge, skills, or financial stability, maybe you draw inspiration from this person because of their beliefs and what they stand for morally or ethically.

There are many reasons to surround yourself with certain people. Ethics, values, power, talent, courage—the list can go on almost indefinitely. It's all about where you want to go, who you want to be, and what you want to achieve.

RIGHT UNDER YOUR OWN ROOF

If you're lucky enough, the first people to serve as role models in your life will be your parents. They're the ones raising you, so it's only natural that you'll look to them for inspiration. You'll probably emulate how they talk, how they walk, and how they conduct themselves in different situations. Now, depending on who your parents are, that can be either a good thing or a bad thing. I definitely had my fair share of encounters at work where I said to myself, "Why the hell is this kid acting like this?" But that question was quickly answered once I saw their parents' behavior. Fortunately, that type of occurrence was a rarity. For every one of those scenarios, I had three positive experiences where a child did the right thing, and when I met their parents, I could tell that the apple hadn't fallen far from the tree.

In the modern world, it's relatively common to see a child brought up in a single-parent home. So the responsibility for setting a good example falls solely on the shoulders of the mother or father. Although my childhood was slightly different, I was also a kid who grew up admiring one parent. In my case, it was my mother. My mom gave birth to me when she was only eighteen years old, and to my brother when she was nineteen. She then had my sister two years later. You may be thinking, "Wow, that's a lot of kids to have by twenty-two years old." And you have the right to think that, but her experience was a common story. She

245

was married to my father and thought that they would be together forever. Things didn't work out the way she had planned, and my father decided he wasn't ready for a family, so he left.

But my mom didn't have that option. She now had three small children and a very limited income. As you can imagine, it wasn't easy. It's funny to think about now, but I can remember a few of the different places that we lived, and for us, it was an upgrade to go from an apartment with cockroaches to a place with mice. As a kid I would lie in my bed at night and listen to the mousetraps snap as they caught our unwanted pets. It got to the point where I was so used to the sound that it no longer woke me up.

We moved around a lot, but my mom continued to work hard and eventually found a nice apartment right next to my grandparents. For my siblings and me, our grandmother and grandfather were a huge part of our lives and became like second parents. They watched us while my mom worked, and they provided us with a little more structure. Although they were a huge help, our fate as a family was still ultimately my mother's responsibility.

A few years later, she met my stepfather, and he provided the discipline we were lacking and also got us involved in sports. They eventually decided to have a child together, and my mom gave birth to my younger sister. We were a large family, but my parents always made sure we never went without. I will always love and respect my stepfather for coming into our lives and taking on a huge responsibility. With that said, no one has been there for me more than my mother.

She missed out on a lot of things, including going to college, hanging out with friends, and traveling. That entire portion of her life was over before it started, but I never once heard her complain. She worked tirelessly for us, and although we didn't have a lot, we always had what we needed. I watched her struggle to pay the bills, but when Christmastime came, we always had presents. And when the new school year started, we didn't go on a big shopping spree, but she was still able to buy us some new clothes.

It wasn't about what she bought for us or the places we lived. She provided a sense of trust and security. I knew that no matter where I was or what I was going though, my mom had my back. She always put her kids before herself, and she still does. Throughout my life up to the present day, if I call my mom and ask for help, it's not "Is there anybody else who can do it?" or "I'm busy right now." The first words out of her mouth have always been "I'm on my way."

I didn't realize it when I was young, but my mother's constant display of selflessness molded me into the person I am today. She was able to teach me what it means to be a parent in the only way it can be taught: by showing me. Her actions while I was a child inspired me to do the same for my children as an adult. She put aside her personal ambitions to provide a better life for her children. Her dedication to her family is something that motivates me to do whatever I can to make sure that my family never goes without, even if it's at my own expense. My mother showed me that it's not about the material things you can provide; it's about being present. It's being there when your children need you and the willingness to do whatever it takes to make sure you never let them down.

If I could accomplish one goal as a parent, it would be to have my children look back at their childhood and speak of me the same way I now talk about my mother.

SCHOOL'S IN SESSION

Not everyone is fortunate enough to have a role model at home. And even if they do, they may be searching for additional inspiration. Teachers have an opportunity to fill that void, but the choice is up to them.

Some educators choose to focus strictly on the main purpose of their job—English, math, science, history...the fundamentals. That's where it starts and ends for them. Then there are teachers who, in addition to educating, invest time in building relationships. Instead of focusing only on curriculum, they devote time to the social element of a teacher-student relationship. It may be as simple as asking the student about their day, or it could be as involved as spending time with them outside of the classroom.

Although the amount of effort needed to interact with a student on a personal level may be minimal, it can often have a profound effect on shaping a young mind.

For all the teachers who are reading this book, as a parent I would like to say "Thank you." I'm well aware of the lasting influence a teacher can have on a student's life. You spend a large portion of the day with our children and play an integral role in not only their education, but their development as a person. I have the utmost respect for your position, and although it may be a thankless job at times, please know that we appreciate what you do.

As I told you earlier, when I was in the fifth grade, I had really lost my way. After meeting Matt, I started turning things around, and I wanted to continue as I entered the sixth grade. Fortunately for me, I was placed in a class with the perfect teacher. His name was Mr. Grenier, and he was a young, smart, charismatic guy. In addition to being a skilled and compassionate teacher, he was also a well-known baseball coach, and he owned one of the most prestigious baseball academies in the state. I was just starting to take a serious interest in baseball, so having him as a teacher was just one more reason for me to do well.

Mr. Grenier knew that I was struggling with school, and that he had the power to send me back to the fifth grade with the stroke of a pen. I remember him pulling me aside after class one day to have a very candid conversation.

He told me straight out, "You know you're *not* failing this class, right?" I didn't know what to say, so he continued. "I know you like to push your teacher's buttons, but that ain't happening with me. You're going to do what I ask, and you're going to do it the right way. I'm not letting you take the easy way out, and if you try to half-ass it, I'm going to call you on it."

By the look on his face, I knew he wasn't joking. But I also understood that he wasn't trying to intimidate me. He was setting the tone in a way that was designed to keep me on track. A kid like me needed that, or I would try and take advantage of every situation that I could. Somehow, he knew that, and he put an end to it before it even started.

I can tell you that the sixth grade was the first year I took an actual interest in my schoolwork. Not only was I doing it for myself, I also didn't want to disappoint Mr. Grenier. I'll admit that I had a few relapses during the year, but he would always pull me aside and speak his mind. Sometimes he was disappointed, and sometimes he was outright pissed off. I looked up to him, and when he spoke to me, it felt like more than just a teacher reprimanding his student. I could tell that he was genuinely upset, which made me feel even worse. I didn't enjoy feeling like I had let him down, and that emotion served as a strong deterrent when I felt like giving up on the tasks he assigned.

Mr. Grenier had a certain level of expectation for me. He

didn't want me to complete a project with a halfhearted effort; he expected it to be the best one in the class, and when it wasn't, he was hard on me. He never let me slide. If I didn't live up to the standards he had set for me, he would make me do it all over again until I got it right. That was probably the most important character trait I took away from my time with Mr. Grenier—the unwillingness to settle for second best. He inspired me to do better and work harder at everything I did until I had reached or surpassed my own expectations. I ended up doing very well that year, and I finished as one of the top students in my class. Right before graduating, Mr. Grenier rewarded my performance with an invitation to attend his baseball academy—for free.

A few years later, I had the chance to give back. I worked as a park supervisor with a group of kids who had a very similar upbringing to mine. Their parents would drop them off during the day and leave them there until it was time for me to leave. They basically used the park as a free daycare service, but I didn't mind. I loved the kids and the fact that they looked up to me. It was an opportunity for me to have the type of impact on them that Mr. Grenier had on me. I took the time to get to know them, and I always pushed them to do their best. I worked at the park for almost six years, so I got to watch many of them grow up and mature into responsible young adults. I would still see some of them while patrolling the streets of Central Falls. Now they have kids of their own, and although they're adults, I take pride in the fact that most of them still remember me. It's an affirmation that I must have done something right, and hopefully I played a small part in inspiring them to do more with their own lives.

The point of this story is simple. Your role models *can* come from outside the home, and oftentimes they will consist of the people you spend a significant amount of time with. Because you're with them so often, they'll be more candid with you, which can sometimes feel like they're coming down on you, but make no mistake about it: they're hard on you because it's their responsibility to challenge you. Consider these individuals, especially the good ones, as professional mentors. Seek out their inspirational direction and let yourself benefit from the life lessons they're willing to teach you.

THE BIG PICTURE

When setting your sights on an aggressive goal and looking for inspiration to help you get there, it's okay to look beyond the people you personally know to find what you need. If you want to discover your full potential, you need to push beyond your own limits. The most effective way to do that is by choosing someone who is the best at what *they* do. If you think about it, why would you shadow the runner-up when you can follow in the footsteps of the champion?

Choosing accomplished individuals as inspiration is something that most of us already do in one way or another. At times, it's an unconscious choice, where we find ourselves fascinated with a particular person. Other times, we make a conscious decision to emulate someone we admire. For some of us it's a professional athlete; for others it's a wealthy entrepreneur. Depending on what you're trying to achieve, the people who will have the most influence on your life will vary. And diversity is a good thing. It allows you to choose the right person for your current mission.

Intelligence, creativity, power, and wealth are qualities that most people desire for themselves. And trust me, I'm no exception. Have you ever envisioned yourself driving a new Lamborghini like Jamie Foxx? Or living in a huge mansion like Oprah? Or having as much money as billionaire Mark Cuban? We've all imagined what it would be like to be in their shoes, to have their financial stability and personal possessions. But let me ask you a question. Is just *wanting* what they have inspirational? I personally don't think so. These individuals are extremely talented and should be recognized for much more than their wealth. When most people think about successful celebrities, athletes, and entrepreneurs, they usually concentrate on the rewards that came with their success, not what they *did* to earn them.

Take Elon Musk for example, a visionary who is always looking to push the limits of human capability and accomplish the impossible. Most people admire him because of his successful businesses and estimated net worth of fourteen billion dollars. But what's even more admirable than Musk's economic status is how he got there and the motivation behind his achievements. The main focus of all his enterprises is to change the world and humanity for the better. Tesla Motors, SpaceX, and now SolarCity—all business that seek to improve our way of living while simultaneously reducing the negative effects we have on the environment.

As of April 2016, Facebook is estimated to be worth around $350 billion, putting creator Mark Zuckerberg's net worth around $56 billion.[19] But that shouldn't be the main reason why you aspire to be like him. People like Zuckerberg are inspirational not only because of their lucrative businesses, but also their generosity and philanthropic efforts. Mark and his wife, Priscilla Chan, live a modest lifestyle when you consider their status, and they have pledged to donate 99 percent of their net worth to the Chan Zuckerberg Initiative, an organization devoted to advancing human potential and equality.

The Zuckerbergs and Elon Musk are the types of individuals worth watching. Both are living examples of the best that humanity has to offer. They see beyond their own interests to the world at large, and employ their wealth and power to benefit those around them. That higher level of drive, determination, and generosity… *that's* what inspires me.

In addition to public figures in sports, business, art, and industry, we can also find inspiration from the lives of some of the more notable leaders in history. When you think about how the founders of the United States worked together to create a set of principles that still serve as the standard more than two hundred years later, that's impressive. I appreciate and respect the work that people like Alexander Hamilton, Thomas Jefferson, and Ben Franklin carried out for our country. They understood that they were acting not just for themselves, but for posterity. They always kept their focus on the bigger picture. The Constitution. Congress. The shape and fabric of our government—that was their main priority.

There have also been influential people, like Abraham Lincoln, Harriet Tubman, and Martin Luther King Jr., who invoked change and altered the makeup of our society through their actions. They were fearless. They were courageous. They knew that what they represented was bigger than themselves, and some of them paid for it with their lives. That kind of selflessness and vision, which shifted the course of this country and made America a place where everyone can pursue their dreams, is truly inspirational.

Throughout this book, we have mainly focused on how to jump-start your career and your personal life. But we have to round out the conversation with the consideration that self-serving behavior can limit your potential. You can't do everything alone. If you really want to reach your maximum potential, you have to look beyond yourself. You have to create an army before you can win the war, and that requires building up and supporting the individuals around you.

You know what smart people do to increase their success? They surround themselves with even smarter people. And as we've already discussed, you don't have to personally know these individuals to take a play from their playbook. You have the ability to pull different components from all of your mentors, creating an approach that is specific to you but already proven effective through your mentors' personal and professional achievements. Use what you've learned to grow as an individual, but also ensure that your efforts contribute to something bigger than yourself.

TRAGEDY CAN INSPIRE CHANGE

Inspiration isn't only derived from people; it can also be found in the actions around us. It doesn't always have to be an over-the-top display of heroism; it can be something as simple as having the courage to do what's right, even when it's not the easiest option.

I worked in an environment where it was pretty common to see someone risk their life for the sake of someone else. Even though this is expected of a police officer, that doesn't make it any less heroic or inspirational. However, seeing police officers and firemen run toward danger when everyone else is running away is not the only inspiration I found at work. One of the unfortunate things about my job was that I usually saw people at their worst. If you're calling the police, it's not to invite us to a party or see how we're doing; it's because you need our help. But there were sometimes when I left an incident feeling like I gained some positive perspective.

When I was still a patrolman, I responded to a domestic disturbance call between a boyfriend and girlfriend. I had maybe three years on the job at this time. When I got there, I learned that the actual issue was between the woman's fifteen-year-old son, Elias, and her boyfriend. Elias was extremely upset, so I pulled him aside and asked him to explain what had happened. He was crying and punching things. He wouldn't even look at me. All he kept saying was that he didn't want to talk about it, because I wasn't "going to do shit anyway." I grabbed him, looked him right in the eyes, and told him to calm down and tell me what had happened. He responded with the same attitude: "What's the point?"

I lowered my voice so only he could hear me and said, "Because I want to help you, and I'm not leaving here until I do."

He paused for a moment to size me up. He was trying to figure out if I was being genuine or not. After a few seconds, he let down his guard and told me that his mom's boyfriend was always hitting him, so tonight he decided to hit back.

I saw a lot of myself in Elias, and I understood what he was going through. Instead of trying to convince him that it wasn't that bad, I did what had been done for me when I was his age: I told him the truth. I explained to him that his current situation wasn't that great and that he hadn't been dealt the best hand. But if he wanted to change his life, he had to start making the right choices.

Then I wrote my phone number down on a blank page in my notebook, ripped it out, and handed it to him. I told him that if he still wanted to hit something tomorrow, he should give me a call. You should've seen his face. He wasn't expecting my reaction and was dumbfounded that I had not only acknowledged that his life wasn't perfect, but was also willing to help him fix it.

When he finally realized that I was looking out for him, he packed a few things and went to his friend's house for the night. The next afternoon, Elias did call me, and I had him meet me at a local boxing gym in the city. I hooked him up with one of the trainers and told him that if he stuck with it, I would come see his first fight.

Elias ended up falling in love with boxing, and a little over a year later, I got the call. I attended his first official fight, and it was really gratifying to see a troubled kid use his frustration for something positive. The result? Elias turned out to be one hell of a fighter.

After the fight, Elias pulled me aside and told me that he had written me a message on Facebook and wanted me to read it when I got home. In his message, he explained how much it meant to him that I was willing to help out at a time when he thought that he was alone. He ended the message by saying, "Thank you. You made me the man I am today." Here I was, a troubled kid myself who had a few people help me along the way, now on the other side of the fence. It was unfamiliar territory, but it inspired me to want to do more.

Elias and I kept in touch, and our relationship grew stronger as he got older. I always made an effort to check in on him. We'd get together for soccer games, or I'd invite him over for dinner so we could catch up. Time passed and our lives changed, and we gradually stopped seeing each other as much. I was working a lot, and he was concentrating on boxing. The phone calls and text messages became less frequent.

But then I got the call that nobody wants. Elias was dead. He had been having some issues that I wasn't aware of, and decided to take his own life. To make matters worse, I found out that only hours before killing himself, he actually came to the police station to talk with me. Unfortunately, I wasn't working that day, and no one ever called.

Although this was a tragic set of circumstances, I still found a source of inspiration in Elias's death. It reinforced the importance of never taking a friendship for granted. It isn't enough to build a strong relationship; you have to continuously work at it. I had lost sight of that. And I still find myself wondering what I might have been able to do if Elias and I had talked more often. Even though I'll never know the answer to that question, the loss of his life

259

lingers in my head as a constant reminder to keep in touch with the people I care about. In the end, Elias inspired me to not only be a better friend, but a better person.

I know what you're saying: "Jesus, Derrick. I thought this story was supposed to be inspiring!" Truth is, not all inspirational occurrences have a happy ending. I would even make the argument that some of the most inspiring stories are the result of horrible circumstances. Think about all the parents who have children with life-threatening diseases or disabilities. They spend the majority of their time in a hospital with their children, not knowing if they'll ever come home. I honestly don't know if I could do it. Their ability to stay positive in what I would consider my worst nightmare is something I can't even fathom. *Those* are the types of people that we should all be drawing inspiration from.

Inspiration can be found almost anywhere. You can see it in a person, or learn it from their actions. You can find it in someone who's part your life or someone you don't even know. Becoming a better person by drawing inspiration from those around you should always be a priority, no matter how successful you become. There's an old saying, *You are the company you keep.* Well, if that's true, I want to be surrounded by the most powerful and influential people I can find. The successful will motivate you to push yourself beyond your own mental boundaries, instilling the internal drive needed to accomplish your mission. The message they convey is simple but impactful. The things *you* want in life are obtainable. If you believe in yourself and work hard enough—nothing is impossible.

EPILOGUE

||||||||||||||||||||||||||||||||||||||||||||||||||||||||

DEBRIEFING

So that's it. We're at the finish line. We've covered a lot of material, and I don't expect you to remember all of it, but I hope you picked up on a few things that help you in the future. As I told you in the introduction, this book doesn't have all the answers—no book does—but life is about progression, and if *this* book helps you grow as a person, then it served its purpose.

No, I'm not a millionaire or a certified life coach. And yes, I'm still relatively young. But I have no problem saying that I've seen and done things that many successful people twice my age haven't experienced. I've had the opportunity to help hundreds of people through circumstances that you'll never personally encounter. That doesn't make me more qualified than anyone else to give you advice. What it does mean is that I might offer some ideas that aren't necessarily traditional but are more effective because *they are different*. And for me, that was the whole point.

I didn't want to offer suggestions to problems that could be found in ten other books. I wanted to bring a new, unconventional style of communication that was innovative but familiar enough to be implemented by anyone.

I get asked a lot about what aspects of my life I consider the most important contributors to my success, and my response is always the same: knowing who you are and clearly defining what you want to accomplish are absolutely essential to achieving your goals. That has always been *my* central focus. So if you choose to concentrate on a few key phrases from this book, please make sure that two of them are *Know yourself* and *Know your target*.

I cannot emphasize enough how important it is to understand your strengths and weaknesses and to know what tools you have at your disposal. And as important as it is to know who *you* are, it's equally important to understand who your target is and what makes *them* tick. This is where your ability to observe really kicks in. Whether it's a romantic interest, a customer, a student, an employer, or an employee, you need to know what they respond to. It's not always about what you're good at; it's figuring out what they find important, identifying the qualities you possess that are in line with their values, and then adapting your approach to highlight those attributes. *That's* the formula for leaving a lasting impression.

When you're constantly pushing the boundaries of your abilities, obstacles are inevitable. You'll find yourself in situations where you feel like there's no solution. I've been there. I know what it feels like to not see the light at the end of the tunnel, to feel claustrophobic in your own mind. Remember that negative thoughts lead to negative outcomes. Instead, choose to believe in the power of positive thinking. Understand that whatever adversity you're facing, there's always a path to resolution, even if you have to create your own.

Mental strength comes from within, but the individuals you surround yourself with are also instrumental to your personal advancement. As a kid, I really didn't trust anyone, so my core group of people was relatively small. As I've gotten older, I've realized the importance of building a team around me. When I need strength or motivation, I think about my family. When I'm indecisive, I seek the opinion of trusted colleagues and friends. And when I'm looking to be inspired, I turn to my mentors. These are the people who make up your foundation. And if you want to continuously move forward, it's imperative that you build a social network around those who represent the same values and ambitions as you. Having people you can rely on will keep you humble in success and determined after a setback.

As a police sergeant, I instilled the same mentality in my officers. I'll be honest, we didn't always get along, but I always reiterated the fact that we were stronger as a unit than we were as individuals. This allowed us to focus on our common interests and set aside our differences. We motivated each other through our unwavering commitment to standing up for what's right and our unwillingness to concede, no matter what the cost.

A team has its benefits, but sometimes, the job requires you to work alone. As an undercover detective, I was put in situations where I had no one to rely on but myself.

I knew that my success would be determined by my ability to observe, adapt, and communicate under stressful situations. I had to know who my target was and become the person they wanted me to be.

I didn't know it at the time, but the approach to undercover work also applies to everyday life. Achieving personal and professional success hinges on your ability to observe and understand your target. By developing a profile, you can use that information to adapt to the situation, communicate more effectively, and accomplish your mission.

That's your undercover edge.

ENDNOTES

||||||||||||||||||||||||||||||||||||||||||||||||||||||||

1   Carl Gustav Jung, *The Archetypes and the Collective Unconscious*, Volume 9, Part 1 of Bollingen Series (Princeton, NJ: Princeton University Press, 1981), 270.

2   "The Johari Window: Using Self-Discovery and Communication to Build Trust," MindTools, accessed March 31, 2017, https://www.mindtools.com/CommSkll/JohariWindow.htm.

3   L. Tozzi et al., "Longitudinal Functional Connectivity Changes Correlate with Mood Improvement after Regular Exercise in a Dose-Dependent Fashion," *European Journal of Neuroscience* 43, no. 8 (2016): 1089–96.

4   Hans Selye, *The Stress of Life* (New York: McGraw Hill, 1976), 420.

5   M Gerber et al., "Increased Objectively Assessed Vigorous-Intensity Exercise Is Associated with Reduced Stress, Increased Mental Health and Good Objective and Subjective Sleep in Young Adults," *Physiology & Behavior* 135 (August 2014): 17–24.

6   Greg LeMond and Mark Hom, *The Science of Fitness: Power, Performance, and Endurance* (New York: Academic Press, 2014), 87.

7   Michael A. Sauter, Charles B. Stockdale, and Douglas A. McIntyre "The 10 Countries Where People Save the Most Money," Fox Business, August 15, 2011, accessed March 16, 2017, http://www.foxbusiness.com/markets/2011/08/15/10-countries-where -people-save-most-money.html.

8   "Schweizer sind Europameister im Sparen" [Swiss Are European Champions in Saving], trans. Derrick Levasseur, *20 Minuten*, July 17, 2013, accessed March 19, 2017, http://www.20min.ch/ finance/news/story/19856163.

9   Suze Orman, "Emergency Fund 101," *Suze Orman* (blog), July 23, 2015, accessed September 2016, http://www.suzeorman.com/ blog/emergency-fund-101/.

10   "The Health Benefits of Strong Relationships," *Harvard Women's Health Watch*, December 2010, accessed April 3, 2017, http://www.health.harvard.edu/newsletter_article/the-health-benefits-of -strong-relationships.

11   James Geary, *Geary's Guide to the World's Great Aphorists* (New York: Bloomsbury, 2008), 262.

12   "Derrick Calls Out Caleb for West Point Lie," YouTube video, 1:07, from an episode of Big Brother, posted by "SMSCentauris," July 3, 2014, https://www.youtube.com/watch?v=2wJyuemWt1k.

13   Pat Williams, *Coach Wooden: The 7 Principles That Shaped His Life and Will Change Yours* (Grand Rapids: Revell, 2011).

14   P. Chadha et al., "A Randomized Control Trial Exploring the Effect of Mental Rehearsal and Cognitive Visualization on Microsurgery Skills," *Journal of Reconstructive Microsurgery* 32, no. 7 (September 2016): 499–505; A. Saimpont et al., "The Comparison between Motor Imagery and Verbal Rehearsal on the Learning of Sequential

Movements," *Frontiers in Human Neuroscience* 18, no. 7 (November 2013): 773.

15 Joe Haefner, "Mental Rehearsal and Visualization: The Secret to Improving Your Game without Touching a Basketball!" *Breakthrough Basketball*, 2008, last modified 2014, accessed April 3, 2017, https://www.breakthroughbasketball.com/mental/visualization. html; Jennifer Cumming and Richard Ramsey, "Imagery Interventions in Sport," *Advances in Applied Sport Psychology: A Review*, eds. Stephen Mellalieu and Sheldon Hanton, (New York: Routledge, 2008), 5–36.

16 Terry Cralle and W. David Brown, *Sleeping Your Way to the Top* (New York: Sterling, 2016), 51.

17 Daniel Todes, *Ivan Pavlov: Exploring the Animal Machine* (New York, NY: Oxford University Press, 2000), 51.

18 Saul McLeod, "Skinner—Operant Conditioning," *Simply Psychology,* last modified 2015, accessed March 18, 2017, http://www.simplypsychology.org/operant-conditioning.html.

19 Noah Kirsch, "Mark Zuckerberg Makes $1.6 Billion in a Week, Net Worth Soars to All-Time High," Forbes, October 22, 2016, accessed April 3, 2017, https://www.forbes.com/sites/noahkirsch/2016/10/22/mark-zuckerberg-net-worth-facebook-record/#5d890ea02cb2.

ACKNOWLEDGMENTS

First off, I want to thank all of the people I've mentioned throughout this book. In one way or another, you've had a lasting impact on my life and for that, I am extremely grateful.

To my wife Jana, thank you for your love and support. I know I've come up with some crazy ideas, but you've never deterred me from pursing my dreams. Writing this book was a big undertaking, and I couldn't have done it without you. I cannot thank you enough for your selflessness and willingness to hold down the fort while my head was buried in a laptop.

To Tenley and Peyton—you're too young to read this now, but you won't always be. You are the ultimate inspiration for this book. I can't tell you how many times I've envisioned walking into a bookstore with both of you and seeing this book on the shelf. I want you to know that nothing is impossible if you want it badly enough, and I hope that this book serves as a constant reminder.

I also would like to thank my parents, Gerard and Sue, for raising me right—even though I didn't always make it easy. To my brother Matt and my sisters Meaghan and Aimee—I appreciate the support system you've provided during my unconventional ventures.

I want to thank my mother-in-law, Stephanie Donlin, for taking the time to read every chapter and giving me your honest opinion, even when I didn't want to hear it.

Pat Rogan—thanks for brainstorming with me on the plane ride home from Arizona. Your ideas and enthusiasm about the possibility of this book motivated me to start writing as soon as we landed.

Many thanks go to my literary agent, Steve Harris of CSG Literary Partners, for taking me on as a client, believing in what I had to say, and for introducing me to Michael Christian. Mike, you helped me to become a better writer, and you challenged me to push my abilities. Thank you for serving as a mentor throughout this entire process.

I am so appreciative of the entire team at Sourcebooks, especially Anna Michels, who took a chance on a first-time writer and allowed me to share my story. I also want to thank Grace

Menary-Winefield for stepping up and taking on a project that was already underway. Your knowledge and professionalism throughout the editing process was outstanding.

Finally, I would like to address all of my supporters, especially those who have been with me since I appeared on *Big Brother*. I see all of your emails, tweets, comments, and posts. Your encouragement is what suppresses my fear of failure and allows me to creatively express myself in ways I never thought possible. Thank you for giving me the opportunity to share my life with you. Hopefully, this is just the beginning.

ABOUT THE AUTHOR

Derrick Levasseur is a retired police sergeant from Central Falls, Rhode Island. Hired at only twenty years old, he is one of the youngest officers in the department's history and has worked in both the Patrol Division and the Detective Division. Due to his street smarts and communication skills, he worked as an undercover detective for the Special Investigations Unit, which resulted in numerous arrests and seizures. In addition to his experience in the field, he has advanced training in crime scene analysis, interview and interrogation techniques, and undercover operations. Throughout the course of his career, Derrick received multiple awards, including letters of recognition, unit citations, commendations, and the Medal of Valor, which is the highest honor a sworn officer can receive.

Before becoming a police officer, Derrick received an associate's degree in criminal justice from Mitchell College. He eventually returned to school and earned his bachelor's degree in criminal justice from Roger Williams University and a master's degree in business management from Salve Regina University.

Based on his life experiences, education, and law enforcement background, Derrick developed an innovative approach to communicating with people in both his personal and professional life. This assisted him in building stronger relationships and achieving personal goals. He decided to put his unconventional but practical approach to the test in a real-life social experiment on CBS's hit series *Big Brother*. Based on the results, he is now regarded as one of the greatest players to have ever played the game. He is the only player out of all past winners to have won the game without ever being nominated for eviction and currently holds the record for the highest total earnings ($575,000) of any contestant in the show's history.

Derrick also starred in Investigation Discovery's hit docuseries, *Is O.J. Innocent? The Missing Evidence*, a program that gave viewers a firsthand look at his investigative style and interviewing techniques.

In addition to appearing on television and speaking at public events, Derrick hopes that this book will further help people to develop a stronger understanding of how to use observation, adaptation, and communication to succeed in their own lives.

To learn more about Derrick and his future projects, follow him on Twitter at @DerrickL and on Instagram at @DerrickVLevasseur. Visit his website at OfficialDerrick.com.